BINGHAM'S MOTOR CLAIMS CASES

BINGHAM'S MOTOR CLAIMS CASES

SUPPLEMENT TO
SEVENTH EDITION

BY

J. A. TAYLOR, LL.B. (LOND.)
SOLICITOR

LONDON
BUTTERWORTHS
1976

ENGLAND:	BUTTERWORTH & CO. (PUBLISHERS) LTD. LONDON: 88 KINGSWAY, WC2B 6AB
AUSTRALIA:	BUTTERWORTHS PTY. LTD. SYDNEY: 586 PACIFIC HIGHWAY, CHATSWOOD, NSW 2067 ALSO AT MELBOURNE, BRISBANE, ADELAIDE AND PERTH
CANADA:	BUTTERWORTH & CO. (CANADA) LTD. TORONTO: 2265 MIDLAND AVENUE, SCARBOROUGH M1P 4S1
NEW ZEALAND:	BUTTERWORTHS OF NEW ZEALAND LTD. WELLINGTON: 26/28 WARING TAYLOR STREET, 1
SOUTH AFRICA:	BUTTERWORTH & CO. (SOUTH AFRICA) (PTY.) LTD. DURBAN: 152/154 GALE STREET

ISBN 0 406 11807 8

PREFACE

This supplement adds about one hundred and thirty cases to the seventh edition of *Bingham's Motor Claims Cases*.

On a subject so essentially empirical as motor claims the dividing line between questions of law and questions of fact is sometimes scarcely discernible. Nevertheless reported decisions of fact can be of help when dealing with similar cases: as, for example, a driver's duty of care to child pedestrians (p. A5) or to people who walk in the roadway at night (pp. A7–A8). The wearing of seat belts has received much judicial attention. When this edition went to press in December 1972 only one English decision on that issue had been reported. In the course of the next two and a half years a dozen cases appeared in the reports exhibiting a remarkable division of opinion among the judges whether or not failure to wear a seat belt called for a reduction of damages (pp. A15–A18). In July, 1975, the question came at last before the Court of Appeal (*Froom* v. *Butcher* pp. A18–A19) and the answer was, for the time being at least, put beyond doubt.

Among new statutes the most notable is the Limitation Act 1975 (pp. A40–A43). This act in language of perhaps deceptive simplicity sweeps into oblivion problems, difficulties and hard cases arising from the 1954 and 1963 Acts, but may well in its turn produce some surprising results when the width of its provisions has been fully realised.

Reported cases on damages proliferate, including a sad number where a plaintiff has sustained catastrophic injuries causing total and lifelong incapacity (pp. A27–A30). The assessment of damages in such cases has become increasingly complex, the more so because of the requirement that components of the award shall be separately assessed (see *George* v. *Pinnock*, p. A27). A significant comment for the future came from the Master of the Rolls in *Taylor* v. *Bristol Omnibus Co.* (p. A30): "These huge lump sums give food for thought. Our present system of assessing and awarding compensation for injuries such as these calls for radical re-appraisement; and I hope that the Royal Commission presided over by Lord Pearson will do this".

November, 1975. J.A.T.

TABLE OF CONTENTS

TABLE OF STATUTES

References in this Table to *"Statutes"* are to Halsbury's Statutes of England (Third Edition) showing the volume and page at which the annotated text of the Act will be found.

LIST OF CASES

The page number refers to the case name given at the *end* of the case summary.

NOTER-UP

The page numbers in bold type in the left-hand margin refer to the pages of the main volume.

PAGE

7 After Connelly v. Hemphill add.—

Snowdon and Ashton were acquainted with each other by being members of the same football team. Ashton asked Snowdon, who owned a car, to teach him to drive but Snowdon declined. When at a club together on the evening of that day Ashton asked Snowdon to lend him the key of his car, which was parked nearby, so that he could sit in it with a girl he had met. Ashton said expressly he did not want to drive the car. Snowdon lent him the key which was also the ignition key. When Ashton and the girl were in the car Ashton decided to drive it and, losing control, crashed it, severely injuring the girl. She sued Snowdon saying he should have realised Ashton might drive off in the car and was thereby negligent, knowing Ashton had not learned to drive. The judge accepted Snowdon's evidence that it never crossed his mind that Ashton would drive.

HELD: Snowdon was not liable. The test was: would a reasonable man in all the circumstances have realised that there was a real risk of Ashton driving the car? The answer was no; Snowdon had no reason to anticipate that Ashton would do something contrary to what he had promised and which would be in more than one respect a criminal offence.

Setchell v. Snowdon,
[1974] R.T.R. 389 (C.A.)

17 Add to the note following Letang v. Cooper.—

Section 2(1) of the 1954 Act has been replaced by s. 2A of the Limitation Act 1939 contained in s. 1 of the Limitation Act 1975, preserving the phrase "breach of duty" (see below, p. A40).

20 After Daniel v. Rickett, Cockerell add.—

The plaintiff, injured in a factory accident, was held by the judge to have been negligent and his damages were reduced by 25%. On appeal counsel submitted that even if the plaintiff was negligent it was not "just and equitable" on the facts to reduce the damages.

HELD: the words of s. 1(1) of the Law Reform (Contributory Negligence) Act 1945 do not entitle a court which has found a plaintiff guilty of contributory negligence to disregard that negligence and make no deduction in the damages on the ground that it would be "just and equitable" not to do so.

Boothman v. British Northrop,
(1972), 13 K.I.R. 112 (C.A.)

39 After Cutler v. United Dairies add.—

The defendants organised a race meeting for jalopy cars. The plaintiff's husband took his car and entered his name as a competitor. He brought his wife, child and mother-in-law to the meeting as spectators.

PAGE

39 He competed in a race but during the next race, in which he was not a
cont. competitor, he stood near a post to which the spectator and safety ropes were fastened talking to his family. The ropes were faultily arranged and on being fouled by a car in that race, pulled out the post and caused the plaintiff's husband injuries from which he died. He had seen the notices around the track: "Warning to the Public. Motor racing is dangerous. It is a condition of admission that all persons having connection with the promotion and/or organisation and/or conduct of the meeting are absolved from all liabilities arising out of accidents causing damage or personal injury (whether fatal or otherwise) howsoever caused to spectators or ticketholders".

HELD: (1) the deceased was at the time of the accident a spectator not a competitor; (2) the defence of *volenti non fit injuria* was available only against one who had impliedly agreed, with full knowledge of the nature and extent of the risk, to incur it. It was not obvious to the deceased that he was standing in a particularly dangerous place and the defence of *volenti* did not apply; (3) the warning notice applied to the deceased as a spectator at the time of the accident and the action failed.

White v. Blackmore,
[1972] 2 Q.B. 651; [1972] 3 All E.R. 158; [1972] 3 W.L.R. 296; 116 S.J. 547 (C.A.)

44 **After Bowater v. Rowley Regis add.—**

The plaintiff, a lighterman, was on his employers' barge waiting to enter the defendants' dock when, by reason of the defendants' negligence, he was hit on the head by a rope which parted. The defendants relied upon a notice which the plaintiff admittedly knew of: "Lightermen . . . availing themselves of the facilities and assistance of the servants of the [defendants] in bringing their craft into and through the entrance of the dock must do so at their own risk . . ."

HELD: the considerations relevant to the defence of *volenti non fit injuria* were correctly set out in BENNETT V. TUGWELL (main volume, p. 45) but in that case and in other motor car cases the plaintiff had a choice whether to ride in the car or not. In the present case the plaintiff was an employee sent by his employer with a barge to this place. It would be wrong to infer that the plaintiff had freely and voluntarily undertaken to incur the risk; he had no free choice. The defence of *volenti non fit injuria* failed.

Burnett v. British Waterways Board,
[1972] 2 All E.R. 1353; [1972] 1 W.L.R. 1329; 116 S.J. 783 (Waller, J.)

52 **After Shiner v. Webster add.—**

On a country road in the dark a motor-cycle and car collided at a bend. The car driver did not remember anything of the accident; the motor cyclist was killed. Marks and débris on the road and the final positions of the vehicles were the only evidence. The judge said that having examined all the facts and argument as put to the court he was unable to say whether or not (as had been argued) the car was on its offside of the road or not at the moment of impact. He therefore considered the right course to adopt was to apply the BAKER V. MARKET HARBOROUGH principle and hold the parties equally to blame. The motor-cyclist's personal representative appealed.

HELD: the judge was entitled so to hold. What he was saying was that

PAGE

52 it was no more probable that the collision took place on the car driver's
cont. wrong side than that it took place in the centre of the road at the bend. As he was quite unable without independent evidence to say whether it was caused by the negligence of the motor-cyclist rather than of the car driver he was right to divide the blame between them equally.

Howard v. Bemrose,
[1973] R.T.R. 32 (C.A.)

63 **Brown and Lynn v. Western S.M.T. Co., Ltd.: delete final sentence and substitute:—**

Per Lord Cooper: The distance which should separate two vehicles travelling one behind the other must depend upon many variable factors —their speed, the nature of the locality, the other traffic present or to be expected, the opportunity available to the following driver of commanding a view ahead of the leading vehicle, the distance within which the following vehicle can be pulled up, and many other things. The following driver is, in my view, bound, so far as reasonably possible, to take up such a position and to drive in such a fashion, as will enable him to deal successfully with all traffic exigencies reasonably to be anticipated: but whether he has fulfilled this duty must in every case be a question of fact whether, on any emergency disclosing itself, the following driver acted with the alertness, skill and judgment reasonably to be expected in the circumstances.

After Brown and Lynn v. Western S.M.T. Co., Ltd. add.—

The defendant was driving a car behind a van, both travelling at about 20 to 25 m.p.h. The van driver braked suddenly to avoid a large piece of metal which dropped off a lorry in front. The defendant did not see the metal fall, his vision being obstructed by the van, and he had no warning that the van driver was about to make an emergency stop. He braked but was unable to avoid colliding with the back of the van. The prosecution, on a charge of driving without due care, presented it as a matter of settled law that if a driver did not leave sufficient space between himself and the vehicle in front to avoid a collision whatever the circumstances, he was guilty of the offence charged; rules 34 and 35 of the Highway Code (1968) were relied on.

HELD: the proposition could not be accepted. The words of Lord Cooper in BROWN AND LYNN V. WESTERN S.M.T. CO., LTD. (quoted above) indicated a standard to be observed by a following driver appropriate in civil cases. The obligation could not be higher on a criminal charge. In the present case it could not be said the justices were perverse in finding the defendant not guilty of the offence.

Scott v. Warren,
[1974] R. T. R. 104 (Div. Ct.)

The plaintiff was a passenger in a mini-bus being driven about two vehicle lengths behind a large tipper lorry along a road having no crossroads, pedestrian crossings or other interferences. The lorry suddenly stopped for no apparent reason and without warning. The driver of the mini-bus had to brake hard to avoid hitting it and was successful in pulling

PAGE

63 up 6 ft. behind the lorry without his brakes locking. The plaintiff was
cont. thrown forward and ricked her neck.

HELD: the test to be applied was that laid down by Lord Cooper in BROWN AND LYNN V. WESTERN S.M.T. CO., LTD. (main volume, p. 63, quoted above, p. A3). The view expressed in WOOLLER V. LONDON TRANSPORT BOARD (main volume, p. 174) was relevant to the present case. On the facts the driver was not negligent.

Parnell v. Receiver for Metropolitan Police,
[1975] 1 Lloyd's Rep. 492 (C. A.)

The plaintiff was riding her moped in a moving line of traffic. There was a Triumph car ahead of her, and in front of that, a Morris driven by the defendant. The Morris pulled up sharply preparatory to turning right. The Triumph was able to pull up safely without colliding with the Morris but the plaintiff could not pull up in time and in trying to avoid the Triumph collided with it and was injured. The judge held the defendant wholly to blame, saying that the plaintiff was not required to ride her moped on the basis that the defendant was suddenly going to stop and put her and the driver in front in jeopardy.

HELD, ON APPEAL: the judge had failed to express correctly the duty of persons driving in a line of traffic; it was to drive at such a distance behind the car in front as to be prepared for foreseeable emergencies. The plaintiff's blame was equal to that of the defendant.

Thompson v. Spedding,
[1973] R.T.R. 312 (C.A.)

The defendant was driving in the dark at about 50 m.p.h. with dipped headlights when his car struck a pedal cyclist travelling in the same direction. The cyclist was in dark clothing and had no rear light on his cycle. The defendant did not see him until within 6 to 8 feet of him. It was contended by the prosecutor on a charge of driving without due care that as the defendant was in breach of rule 34 of Highway Code then by reason of s. 37 (5) of the Road Traffic Act 1972 the defendant was guilty of the offence.

HELD: (1) there was a fallacy in the contention at the outset: the fact that the defendant did not see the cyclist until 6 to 8 feet away did not mean he could not see beyond 8 feet. There were many possible explanations of a failure to see him before he did; (2) whether or not a driver is driving in contravention of s. 3 of the Act must be a question of fact in every case. A breach of rule 34 could have no more positive effect than provided in s. 37(5), namely, that it was evidential. On the facts it could not be said that the justices were perverse in holding that the offence was not proved.

Jarvis v. Fuller,
[1974] R.T.R. 160 (Div. Ct.)

Rule 34 provides: "Never drive so fast that you cannot stop well within the distance you can see to be clear".

68 **After Jones v. Lawrence add.—**

The defendant was driving his car at 25–30 m.p.h. along a street in a poor district in Birmingham on a Sunday afternoon. There was no other traffic. A coach 30 feet long was parked against the nearside

PAGE
68 cont. pavement and concealed from the defendant an opening between the houses on that side of the road just beyond the front of the coach. As the defendant's car was passing the coach the plaintiff, a child of 6, ran from the opening across the front of the coach into the defendant's path and was struck by the nearside front of the car. The judge held the defendant liable: he should have slowed down or sounded his horn.

HELD, ON APPEAL: the defendant was not liable. The test to be applied to the facts was this: would it have been apparent to a reasonable man, armed with commonsense and experience of the way pedestrians, particularly children, are likely to behave in the circumstances such as were known to the defendant to exist in the present case, that he should slow down or sound his horn, or both? What course of action would he have to take if he was going to make quite certain that no accident would occur? Ought he to have slowed down to such an extent that there could have been no possibility of a child's running out at any moment in front of him and his being unable to stop without striking the child? To do so he would have had to slow down to something like 5 m.p.h. Such a duty of care would be unreasonable; the chance that a child would run out at the precise moment he was passing the coach was so slight as not to require him to slow down to that extent. As for sounding the horn, drivers in traffic are constantly exposed to the danger of pedestrians stepping out in front of parked vehicles. It would be an impossible burden for drivers to sound their horns every time they passed a parked vehicle.

Moore v. Poyner,
[1975] R.T.R. 127 (C.A.)

The plaintiff, aged 11½, was struck by the defendant's car when running across the road from the pavement on the defendant's nearside. She had come down a flight of steps to the pavement, which was 3 feet wide. The entrance to the steps was 3 or 4 feet wide. She was struck by the offside front of the car which, after the accident, was parallel with the pavement and 4 feet 9 inches from it. There was a mark on the road behind the nearside rear wheel 22 feet long indicating heavy application of the brakes. The passenger in the nearside front seat of the car saw the plaintiff as she stood momentarily in the entrance to the steps and then dashed across. The defendant did not see her until she was in the act of dashing across; he was then 50 to 60 feet away, travelling at 20 to 25 m.p.h. The judge held him 40% to blame for having failed to see the plaintiff at the moment when his passenger did and failing to sound his horn.

HELD: the fact that the passenger saw the plaintiff a split second before the defendant did not establish a lack of proper care on the defendant's part; he was driving and needed to switch his eyes from one direction to another. Even if he had seen the plaintiff at the same instant it could not be said he should then have sounded his horn; what he did do was to apply his brakes heavily. Having regard to the brake marks he had acted promptly and efficiently. The judge's decision seemed to place a duty on motorists to sound the horn virtually whenever they see a pedestrian, regardless of whether the pedestrian is manifesting an intention of leaving the pavement and dashing across the road. Appeal allowed.

Davies v. Journeaux,
[1975] 1 Lloyd's Rep. 483 (C.A.)

PAGE

70 **Motorway Speed Limits**

S.I. 1971/601 has been replaced by S.I. 1973/748. The general speed limit of 70 m.p.h. on motorways is now contained in S.I. 1974/502.

74 **After note following Clarke v. Winchurch add.—**

The defendants' garage was on the north side of Upper Richmond Road with access by an exit 11 feet wide. Their van was being driven out of the exit across the eastbound traffic stream which was at a standstill. A lorry driver had stopped his vehicle so as to leave a substantial gap and had gestured to the defendants' driver to come out. The plaintiff was riding his motor cycle at about 15 m.p.h. along the offside of the line of traffic, overtaking the stationary vehicles. As the defendants' van came through the gap, turning right, there was a collision between the motor-cycle and the nearside front of the van. The judge held the plaintiff and the van driver equally to blame.

HELD, ON APPEAL: the decision should stand. The plaintiff was doing nothing wrong in overtaking the line of stationary vehicles, but doing that and being aware of this exit and others on to Upper Richmond Road he should have been proceeding with the greatest care and keeping an effective look-out. The van had almost completed its turn when hit and if the plaintiff had been alert he could have swerved away to avoid it. The van driver had to perform a difficult and dangerous manoeuvre and very great care was needed: he should have made quite sure that nobody was going across his path in an easterly direction. It was important to realise that the lorry-driver's gesture merely meant that he was giving way to the van emerging and not that if the van crossed beyond the shelter of the lorry it would be safe. CLARKE V. WINCHURCH (main volume, p. 74) and POWELL V. MOODY (main volume, p. 73) were distinguishable on the facts.

Leeson v. Bevis and Tolchard, Ltd.,
[1972] R.T.R. 373 (C.A.)

77 **Replace note on Williams v. Needham by the following:—**

The plaintiff at night but in a well-lighted street parked her car with its nearside to the kerb so that she could cross to a shop on the other side. She stood in the roadway on the offside of the car with her back to it and looked to her right. She saw nothing approaching and then looked to her left. She saw three cars approaching and waited until they had passed. Then without looking again to her right she stepped forward to cross the road and was at once hit by the defendant's car coming from her right. The defendant had seen her standing by her car looking away from him and had guessed that she intended crossing the road. He assumed she would look to her right before beginning to cross and he took no precautions against her not doing so. When she stepped forward he was too near to avoid hitting her.

HELD: the plaintiff must bear two-thirds of the blame but one-third must rest on the defendant. He knew that people did sometimes begin to cross without looking and, realising the plaintiff was about to cross, should have drawn her attention to the presence of his car or taken some other precautions against the possibility of her taking a risky step.

Williams v. Needham
[1972] R.T.R. 387 (Q.B.D.)

PAGE
79 **After Snow v. Giddins add.—**

Walking on road at night

The plaintiff and a friend were walking along a poorly-lit street at night on the left-hand pavement. From time to time because of snow and slush on the pavement they walked in the roadway near the kerb. Whilst so doing the plaintiff was hit from behind by the defendant's car, which was travelling at speed and did not stop. It was argued for the defendant that the plaintiff was guilty of 25% contributory negligence because she was not complying with the rules for pedestrians in the Highway Code: she was walking next to the kerb with her back to traffic, not wearing or carrying anything white.

HELD: she was not, on the facts, guilty of contributory negligence. Though s. 74(5) of the Road Traffic Act 1960 (now replaced by s. 37(5) of the 1972 Act—main volume, p. 60) enables a party to rely upon a breach of the Highway Code as tending to establish or negative liability, a breach creates no presumption of negligence calling for an explanation, still less a presumption of negligence contributing to causing an accident or injury. A breach is just one of the circumstances on which a party can rely in establishing the negligence of the other and its contribution to causing the accident or injury. It must not be elevated into a breach of statutory duty. In the present case, the plaintiff had not failed to take reasonable care for her own safety in walking a few feet out in the road for about 20 yards when it got too slushy; even if it did amount to negligence it made no real contribution to the accident.

Powell v. Phillips,
[1972] 3 All E.R. 864; 116 S.J. 713 (C.A.)

The defendant was driving his car along a straight unlighted road at night. He saw ahead of him on the nearside of the road two women pedestrians walking in the same direction as he was travelling but failed to see until too late two men walking about 20 yards behind them, the outer about 4′ 6″ from the edge of the road. His car struck both men killing one and seriously injuring the other. The road was 25 feet wide. There was a grass verge on the left of the road but only a hedge on the right. The judge found the defendant wholly to blame. On appeal it was argued that the pedestrians were negligent in not following the advice in the Highway Code to walk on the right of the road so as to face the oncoming traffic.

HELD: there were no grounds for finding contributory negligence. Even if the outside pedestrian was 4′ 6″ out it did not amount to negligence when the road was 25 feet wide. It is depriving pedestrians of their natural rights as highway users to say they must walk on the right and are not entitled to walk on the nearside. The mere fact that a pedestrian walks on the left side of a country road is not necessarily negligent: it depends on the circumstances. In the present case there was a grass verge on the left on to which one could move in an emergency but only a hedge on the right.

Parkinson v. Parkinson,
[1973] R.T.R. 193, n. (C.A., 1963)

PAGE

79 *cont.* The plaintiffs were father and son, the latter aged 13. At night they left the lighted entrance to a fairground adjoining a straight country road and walked along a grass verge alongside the road for a distance and then along the left hand edge of the road for 20 yards or so preparatory to crossing to the other side at a place where there was an isolated street lamp. Before they reached it they were struck from behind by the defendant's car. The judge declined to find the plaintiff father negligent either for his own safety or in respect of his son's.

HELD: the judge was right. Following PARKINSON V. PARKINSON (above) and POWELL V. PHILLIPS (above) a mere contravention of the recommendation in the Highway Code to walk on the right of the road and not to walk with your back to the traffic did not create a presumption of negligence.

Kerley v. Downes,
[1973] R.T.R. 188 (C.A.)

86 **After Hughes v. Hall add.—**

The defendant was driving his car towards an uncontrolled (i.e. "zebra") crossing and was within the area marked by the zig-zag lines when a pedestrian stepped on to the crossing. The defendant continued over the crossing, missing the pedestrian by a foot. On a charge of failing to give precedence he claimed that the area between the zig-zag lines was part of the crossing and that when a vehicle was within the controlled area (i.e. between the zig-zag lines) no pedestrian should move on to the crossing.

HELD: this was a similar contention to that made under the 1954 regulations in HUGHES V. HALL (main volume, p. 86) and was wrong. The roadway between the zig-zag lines was not part of the crossing. If a pedestrian gets on to the striped area before the car gets on to the striped area the driver must give the pedestrian priority.

Moulder v. Neville,
[1974] R.T.R. 53 (Div. Ct.)

93 **After Clark v. Wakelin add.—**

On a busy 3-lane road in daylight a mini van pulled out into the centre lane to overtake a lorry and trailer travelling in the nearside lane. The mini driver whilst still in the centre lane decided to enter a service station on the offside of the road. He put on his offside indicator and braked, slowing down fairly sharply to enter the further of the two entrances; he had already passed the first entrance before braking. The mini van was then struck from behind by a heavily-laden lorry which had been following the mini van in the centre lane. The lorry driver had been about 100 yards behind the mini van when it braked but the driver had not seen the mini's brake light or trafficator. The mini driver was unaware of the presence behind him of the lorry until after the impact.

HELD: the mini driver was engaged in a most undesirable manoeuvre, turning off the centre lane of a fast road into the second entrance of a service station on the offside. It behoved him to make certain he did it without risk to following or oncoming traffic. In the particular circumstances of this case he ought to have given a hand signal; if he had the lorry driver would probably have seen it and avoided a collision. The Highway Code, insofar as it appears to say that hand signals need never

PAGE

93 be used when trafficators and brake lights are in good working order,
cont. contains unwise advice. There may still be circumstances, as in this case, where the utmost warning to other traffic of one's intentions should be resorted to and a hand signal called for. Proportions of blame: mini driver one-third, lorry driver two-thirds.

Goke v. Willett,
[1973] R.T.R. 422 (C.A.)

95 **After Simpson v. Peat add.—**

At night on an unlighted road Williams was driving the first of three cars the other two being driven by friends whom he was leading. He discovered he had taken the wrong route and, seeing a turning on the right, put on his offside flashing indicator preparatory to turning into it so as to go back in the opposite direction. He slowed and moved towards the centre of the road. He looked in his driving mirror when he indicated he was going to turn and looked in the mirror again before he turned. He began to turn into the road on the right without actually stopping; when he was about half-way across the offside half of the road his car was struck by a car driven by Croney which had overtaken both the other cars, Croney not having seen Williams's car ahead until too late. The judge held both drivers equally to blame: he said Williams should have satisfied himself that there was no car overtaking the other two and should have stopped before crossing the offside half of the road.

HELD, ON APPEAL: Williams had done nothing wrong; Croney was wholly to blame.

Challoner v. Williams and Croney,
[1975] 1 Lloyd's Rep. 124 (C.A.)

103 **Speed Limits**

S.I. 1967/1040 and S.I. 1967/1038 have been revoked. The 60 miles per hour and 50 miles per hour (Temporary Speed Limit) Order 1974 imposes a speed limit of 60 miles per hour on any dual carriageway road and 50 miles per hour on any road which is not a dual carriageway road (subject to speed limits imposed by the Road Traffic Regulation Act 1967).

106 **After Gaynor v. Allen add.—**

Fire Engine

On a three-lane road in fog which limited visibility to 50 yards the plaintiff's husband was driving a mini-van in the centre lane, slowly overtaking a lorry and trailer 52 feet long. He was following at least one other car. The defendants' emergency tender (fire engine) was being driven in the opposite direction in the centre lane at 50 m.p.h. with headlights on and blue light flashing. It was taking tools to rescue trapped persons in crashed vehicles some distance away. A car ahead of the tender moved into its nearside lane to let it through, as did the car ahead of the mini. The tender and the mini collided in the centre of the road, killing the plaintiff's husband. It was argued by the defendants that the tender on such an errand could justifiably be driven in a way which in an ordinary vehicle would be regarded as reckless.

HELD: following GAYNOR V. ALLEN (main volume, p. 106) the driver of the tender owed to the public the same duty of care as any other driver: he was negligent in driving too fast in fog and not keeping a

PAGE

106 proper look-out. But the mini driver was the more to blame in the manner
cont. of his overtaking. To overtake as the last of three in a fog is liable to result in an accident. He should have delayed overtaking until he could see what was ahead of him. Instead he was moving forward at a slow differential speed in relation to the lorry he was overtaking and could move neither to right nor left when the tender came in sight. All this happening in a second or two he had placed himself in the worst possible position. He was two-thirds to blame, the defendants' driver one third.

Wardell-Yerburgh v. Surrey C.C.,
[1973] R.T.R. 462 (Brabin, J.)

112 **After note following Sudds v. Hanscombe add.—**

The plaintiff, driving a lorry, approached a cross roads where he intended to turn right. The traffic lights were green for him and changed to amber just as he passed the primary light. He came to a stop in the centre of the junction angled to the right ready to continue to make his turn. He looked to his left and saw the defendant's car approaching about 25 yards away. Knowing the traffic lights had turned to red and seeing the car had time to pull up he began to move forward. The car did not stop but continued on past the red light and collided with the lorry. The County Court judge held the plaintiff 10% to blame for not having apprehended that the car might not stop at the lights.

HELD: on appeal, the plaintiff was not at all to blame. He had good reason to suppose the car would pull up at the traffic signal. Although as Lord du Parcq said in GRANT V. SUN SHIPPING CO. (main volume, p. 4), "a prudent man will guard against the possible negligence of others when experience shows such negligence to be common", one's experience does not lead one to think that it is a common folly for a driver who has time to pull up at traffic lights to fail to do so. The plaintiff was correct in his assessment when he first saw that car that it had time to stop at the lights which were at red and that it was safe for him to move forward.

Hopwood Homes, Ltd. v. Kennerdine,
[1975] R.T.R. 82 (C.A.)

Travelling west along the Great West Road, which has dual 4-lane carriageways, Miss Pouleuf driving a small Citroen wished to turn right at a cross-roads controlled by traffic lights. Having passed the primary light at green she took up a position in the gap between the two ends of the central reservation, at an angle to cross the eastbound carriageway when it should be safe to do so. When the lights changed to amber and red for eastbound traffic three cars slowed down and stopped. A fourth car driven by Evans travelling in the lane nearest the central reservation drove past the red light at speed and collided with the front of the Citroen. The judge held Miss Pouleuf 15% to blame for the collision on the ground that she must have moved forward, having seen the other cars stop and not having seen Evans's car. She strongly denied having moved at all.

HELD, ON APPEAL: (1) on the evidence, Miss Pouleuf had not moved and was not negligent; (2) even if she had moved forward into the path of Evans's car she was not negligent. Knowing from the fact that the other

PAGE

112 cont. cars had stopped that the lights had changed to red for eastbound traffic she was under no duty to look to see if there was traffic in the fourth lane and whether if there were any, it was travelling at such a speed as to be unlikely to stop at the lights. The clear inference of a reasonably careful motorist would have been that there was no reason to think that a car in the fast lane would come across against the lights. HOPWOOD HOMES, LTD. V. KENNERDINE (above) followed. SUDDS V. HANSCOMBE (main volume, p. 112) supported this view.

Miller v. Evans,
[1975] R.T.R. 70 (C.A.)

117 **After Brazier v. Alabaster add.—**

No warning sign

Travelling at 40 m.p.h. or more in the dark a car driven by the defendant entered an S-bend at the end of which was a hump-backed bridge. There was no warning sign of the bridge, which came as a surprise to the defendant. The car lost contact with the road in passing over the bridge and the plaintiff, a passenger, was injured. It was argued for the defendant that he was not to blame for the result of meeting an unsuspected hazard in the road in these circumstances.

HELD: the defendant should have seen the bridge before he hit it even though not warned about it and should have been driving in such a way that, once he did hit the hump he could have controlled the car and so prevented it from leaving the road.

James v. Parsons,
[1975] 1 Lloyd's Rep. 178 (Kilner Brown, J.)

119 **After Walsh v. Redfern add.—**

On a November evening after dark the plaintiffs' car was being driven out of a side street across a main road, which was 26 feet wide and well-lighted, into a street opposite. The main road was a one-way street with traffic travelling only from the car driver's right. As he was about to leave the side street there was on his immediate right against the kerb in the main road a bus which obscured his view to the right. The bus driver gave a flash of his head-lights and a hand signal to the car driver to come on. After looking along the nearside of the bus and seeing nothing approaching the car driver switched on his headlights and drove out slowly across and beyond the front of the bus without stopping. When about to enter the street opposite the car was struck violently on its offside by the defendants' van which had overtaken the bus. The van driver had not seen the car until he was 12 to 15 feet away, nor had he noticed a slow-down signal given by the bus-driver. The judge held the van driver two-thirds to blame for driving at a speed excessive in the circumstances and failing to see the car earlier; he held the car driver one-third to blame for not stopping when the car was just past the bus and when he would have seen the van approaching.

HELD, ON APPEAL: the apportionment should not be disturbed.

Garston Warehousing Co. v. O. F. Smart (Liverpool), Ltd.,
[1973] R.T.R. 377 (C.A.)

PAGE

128 After note following Ready Mixed Concrete v. Min. of Pensions add.—

For a period up to 1968 the appellants, a company which hired out earth-moving machines with drivers, employed Summers as a driver at a weekly wage and on terms which amounted to a contract of service. In that year he asked to be self-employed as a sub-contractor. Thereafter he stamped his own insurance card at the self-employed person's rate, paid his own income tax under Sch. D and was paid at a much enhanced hourly rate, but without travelling allowances, sick pay or provision for holidays. He drove the company's machines as before on sites selected by them under the control of the site foreman or agent. He was not expressly under any duty to work at all but the intention was that he should work exactly as he had before. A determination was made by The Secretary of State for Social Services under the National Insurance Act 1965 that Summers was still a person employed under a contract of service.

HELD: there was no error in law in the Minister's decision.

Global Plant, Ltd. v. Secretary of State,
[1972] 1 Q.B. 139; [1971] 3 All E.R. 385; [1971] 3 W.L.R. 269; 115 S.J. 506 (Lord Widgery, C.J.)

Note: After commenting that "the idea of the degree of control exercised by the employer over the servant being a decisive factor in this question has been very largely modified", Lord Widgery quoted with approval a passage from Cooke, J.'s judgment in MARKET INVESTIGATIONS, LTD. V. MINISTER OF SOCIAL SECURITY, [1969] 2 Q.B. 173; [1968] 3 All E.R. 732; [1969] 2 W.L.R. 1; 112 S.J. 905: "factors which may be of importance are such matters as whether the man performing the services provides his own equipment, whether he hires his own helpers, what degree of financial risk he takes, what degree of responsibility for investment or management he has and whether and how far he has an opportunity of profiting from sound management in the performance of his task".

128 Following N.I.R.C. case add.—

Roberts, a hire-car driver, made an agreement with Davies, who ran a hire-car booking office, having the following elements: Roberts would drive Davies's car for the purpose of carrying passengers who booked in at Davies's Need-a-cab office; Roberts would be on call or attend at the office regularly at agreed times on every weekday except Fridays and Saturdays and would then drive a car as directed by Davies's office; Davies would ensure that Roberts was covered by Davies's own insurance; Roberts would be entitled to 50% of the takings from passengers whom he drove and would pay his own national insurance contributions and income tax.

HELD: the question whether Roberts was employed by Davies under a contract of service or not could be decided by asking: Whose business was it that was being carried on? What they had agreed was that Davies was to supply the car and booking facilities and Roberts was to do the work and they were to split the proceeds 50–50; the answer to the question was that it was the business of both of them. It was not a contract of service, it was a co-adventure.

Roberts v. Warne,
[1973] R.T.R. 217 (Div. Ct.)

PAGE

131 **After Hilton v. Thomas Burton, Ltd. add.—**

The second defendant was a salesman employed by the first defendants. He worked ordinary business hours in his employers' shop in Darlington but was also required to do some canvassing during evenings within the radius of thirty miles, using his own car. Sometimes he went with another salesman, a practice known to their employers which led to better results. One evening he took another salesman Smith on canvassing some distance from Darlington. The canvassing finished by 8 p.m. and they then called at one or more public houses for food and drink. On the way home there was an accident at about 9.30 p.m. caused by the second defendant's negligence.

HELD: the employers were vicariously liable. On the evidence the second defendant was under a duty as an employee to bring his fellow-salesman back to Darlington and was therefore doing something which he was employed to do.

Elleanor v. Cavendish Woodhouse, Ltd.,

[1973] 1 Lloyd's Rep. 313 (C.A.)

134 **After note following Bayley v. M.S. & L. Rly. Co. add.—**

In the course of a bus journey the conductor, a servant of the appellant bus company, spoke sharply to a lady passenger and was reproved for doing so by another passenger, the respondent. An altercation then broke out between the conductor and respondent in which they aimed blows at each other, but they were separated by other passengers. Later, whilst collecting fares, the conductor abused the respondent, using a very rude Chinese expression. The respondent stood up, told the conductor not to use the expression and sat down again. The conductor then hit him with the ticket-punch causing serious injury to his eye. The respondent was awarded damages against the appellants as vicariously liable for the conductor's act on the ground that he was acting, even though in a high-handed manner, in the course of his duty to keep order among the passengers.

HELD, ON APPEAL TO THE PRIVY COUNCIL: the appellants were not vicariously liable. To describe the conductor's act as quelling disorder was impossible on the evidence; if anyone was keeping order in the bus it was the passengers. The evidence fell far short of establishing an implied authority in the conductor to take violent action where none was called for, nor was there present in the bus an emergency situation calling for forcible action justifiable upon any express or implied authority with which the appellants could be said on the evidence to have clothed him.

Keppel Bus Co., Ltd. v. Sa'ad bin Ahmad,

[1974] 2 All E.R. 700; [1974] 1 W.L.R. 1082; [1974] R.T.R. 504 (P.C.)

137 **After Mulholland v. William Reid add.—**

The plaintiff, a bus driver employed by the defendants, found he could not get his bus out of the garage to begin work until the bus behind it had been moved. He asked his conductor, Carberry, to get someone from the engineering department to move the other bus. Instead, Carberry, who had never driven a bus before, tried to move it himself. He started it and it crushed the plaintiff, who was standing between it and his own bus. There was a clear instruction, adequately published, "In no circumstances is a conductor allowed to drive a bus".

PAGE

137 HELD: the defendants were not vicariously liable for Carberry's
cont. negligence. It was not a case within the principle set out in *Salmond on Torts* (quoted in CANADIAN PACIFIC RLY. V. LOCKHART, main volume at p. 136) of his having improperly done what he was authorised to do. The defendants' prohibition did not merely deal with conduct within the sphere of employment; it was a prohibition which limited the sphere of his employment.

Iqbal v. London Transport Executive.
The Times June 7, 1973 (C.A.)

145 **After Conway v. George Wimpey add.—**

The second defendant employed the first defendant as a milkman. Notices at the depot made it clear that roundsmen were not allowed to take children on vehicles. Despite this the first defendant took the plaintiff, a boy of 13, on his milk float, paying him a few shillings for help in delivering milk. Whilst being carried on the vehicle the plaintiff was injured by the first defendant's negligence.

HELD, ON APPEAL (Lawton, L.J. dissenting): there was vicarious liability on the second defendants. This was not a case like TWINE V. BEAN'S EXPRESS and CONWAY V. WIMPEY (main volume, pp. 144 and 145) where lifts were given for the purpose of the employers. The plaintiff was (*per* Lord Denning) doing what was part of the milkman's, and thus the employers', business. Alternatively (*per* Scarman, L.J.) the milkman had chosen to enlist the assistance of a small boy in disregard of the employers' instructions and had thus betrayed their trust. As between morally blameless people he who had put the action in motion should be liable.

Rose v. Plenty
(1975), 119 S.J. 592 (C.A.)

Leave was given to appeal to the House of Lords.

164 **Replace Launchbury v. Morgans by the following.—**

Mrs. Morgans, the defendant, owned a car which was registered and insured in her name. Both she and her husband regularly used it, he more than she. She regarded it as being their car jointly, rather than hers. He used it for going to work. One evening he telephoned her from his place of work, saying he was going out for the evening. He visited various public houses and at one of them, conscious that he ought not to drive, asked a friend named Cawfield to act as his chauffeur for the rest of the evening. Later he and Cawfield left a public house in the car with the plaintiffs as passengers and were travelling to a town some miles away, not in a homeward direction, when an accident occurred due to Cawfield's negligent driving. The defendant's husband and Cawfield were killed, the plaintiffs injured. The defendant had been promised by her husband that if ever he had had too much to drink when out with the car he would get someone who was sober to drive. The Court of Appeal held the defendant vicariously liable for Cawfield's negligent driving on the grounds (*inter alia*) that it was a "family car" and that she had an "interest and concern" in the purpose for which it was being driven.

HELD: allowing the appeal, there was no authority for accepting the "interest and concern" or "family car" arguments, which have no

PAGE

164 *cont.* validity in English law. An owner's vicarious liability for the negligence of the driver was correctly and accurately stated by MacKinnon, L.J., and du Parcq, L.J., in HEWITT V. BONVIN (main volume, pp. 162–163). The understanding between Mr. and Mrs. Morgans that when unfit he would get someone else to drive was no basis for holding that Cawfield had been delegated to drive as agent for her, and she was not vicariously liable for his negligence.

Morgans v. Launchbury
[1973] A.C. 127; [1972] 2 All E.R. 606; [1972] 2 W.L.R. 1217; 116 S.J. 396 (H.L.)

180 **After Hett v. McKenzie add.—**

The defendant's car had seat belts for the front seats, fitted in the usual position on the central door pillar on each side. They were rarely used and were normally left hooked up on each pillar. The plaintiff when being given a lift home by the defendant was travelling in the rear offside seat; at the end of the journey when alighting she caught her foot in the nearside seat belt and fell, sustaining injury.

HELD: the defendant was not liable. On the evidence that the seat belt was probably hooked up the driver was not in breach of duty to the passenger either in allowing it to remain in that condition or failing to warn the plaintiff about it. Even if the belt was not hooked up but was on this isolated occasion lying loose on the floor there was no obligation on the driver to make a visual check or to warn the passenger to make sure the seat belt was satisfactory.

Donn v. Schacter,
[1975] R.T.R. 238 (Phillips, J.)

185 **Following the note after Geier v. Kujawa add.—**

In England the question whether the omission to wear a seat belt was a reason for reducing a plaintiff's damages was argued in a number of cases heard in courts of first instance and gave rise to considerable conflict of opinion among the judges. The question eventually came before the Court of Appeal in FROOM V. BUTCHER (below), decided on July 21, 1975. The following are the cases at first instance:

Damages reduced

By the defendant's admitted negligence his car, in which the plaintiff was a passenger, overturned and the plaintiff was thrown out, suffering injuries which would probably not have been inflicted if he had been wearing the seat-belt. He had worn it at the instance of the defendant (who was wearing his) for 30 miles or so but had neglected to fasten it again after a short stop.

HELD: his damages should be reduced by 25%.

Toperoff v. Mor,
[1973] R.T.R. 419 (Judge Dean, Q.C.)

The plaintiff, aged 19, was a front seat passenger in the defendant's car, not wearing a seat belt, when due to his negligence it struck a lamp-post and she sustained facial injuries by being thrown against the windscreen. She knew of the use of seat belts and had used them in other cars but was unaware that there was one available for her in the defendant's car. He had said nothing about seat belts and was not wearing his.

PAGE

185 cont. The accident took place on a short journey in city streets late at night. Evidence was given by a statistician that the risk of injury was substantially reduced by seat-belts and that there was no difference in this respect between accidents occurring within built-up areas and those outside.

HELD: (1) the plaintiff ought reasonably to have foreseen the possibility of the car being involved in an accident and of her suffering injury as a result; (2) she ought to have found out for herself that the seat-belt was available; (3) it was known to the plaintiff (as enjoined by the Highway Code) that it was sensible to wear seat-belts; (4) there was a clear connection between her failure to wear a seat-belt and the injury she suffered; (5) the defendant's duty of care to the plaintiff involved not merely a duty to drive and control the car with reasonable care and skill but also to take some step towards seeing that the plaintiff wore the seat-belt; since he did nothing to see that she wore it and was in addition careless in driving and controlling the car by far the greater share of overall blame was his. The plaintiff's damages would be reduced by 5%.

Pasternack v. Poulton,
[1973] 2 All E.R. 74; [1973] 1 W.L.R. 476; [1973] 1 Lloyd's Rep. 439 (Q.B.D.)

The plaintiff's husband was killed when thrown from his van after a collision caused entirely by the defendant's negligence. He was not wearing a seat belt: if he had done so he would probably not have been killed.

HELD: the damages should be reduced by one-fifth. A prudent driver guards against the possible negligence of others. A driver in the position of the deceased need not anticipate folly in every form but likewise he was not entitled to reject all the teachings of recent years about the desirability of wearing a seat belt.

Parnell v. Shields,
[1973] R.T.R. 414 (Wien, J.)

Plaintiff, riding as passenger in his employer's car was injured in the face and head by striking the windscreen when the car ran into a stationary vehicle. He had travelled in the same car before and worn a seat belt. He did not wear the cross-brace on this occasion because it was un-uncomfortable. Had he been wearing it he would have sustained no injury at all. Damages reduced by one-third.

McGee v. Francis Shaw & Co., Ltd.,
[1973] R.T.R. 409 (Kilner Brown, J.)

The plaintiff suffered bad facial injuries when a passenger in her husband's car. She may have escaped injury if wearing a seat belt. They were on a short journey in town; she wore a seat belt on a long journey but not on a short one because she thought the risk slight.

HELD: a person travelling in a vehicle on a road is inevitably subject to some risk of injury; the plaintiff ought reasonably to have anticipated injury to herself through any negligence on the part of any driver. CHALLONER V. WILLIAMS, SMITH V. BLACKBURN, CHAPMAN V. WARD (below)

PAGE
185 not followed. She knew it would have been wiser to wear a seat-belt.
cont. Damages reduced by 15%.

Drage v. Smith and Drage,
[1975] 1 Lloyd's Rep. 438 (Judge Stabb)

Damages not reduced

In September 1968 the plaintiff sustained facial injuries in a collision between his car and the defendant's. He was not wearing a seat belt though he sometimes did when travelling at speed.

HELD: a failure to take a safety precaution such as wearing a seat belt can amount to contributory negligence but in the present case (1) it had not been established that in 1968 a prudent motorist would in the circumstances have worn one, and (2) it had not been established that the failure to wear a seat belt caused the injuries.

Lertora v. Finzi,
[1973] R.T.R. 161 (Judge Fay)

Plaintiff injured when a passenger in Williams's car (for facts see Court of Appeal decision, above, p. A9). The defendants were found not to have proved either that the plaintiff was not wearing a seat belt nor that his injuries would have been worse if he had not. *Obiter*, it was unreasonable to require someone to take steps to protect himself against a vague and distant contingency; travelling in a car does not yet involve the incidence of imminent risk to life and limb.

Challoner v. Williams,
[1974] R.T.R. 221 (Shaw, J.)

The plaintiffs, driver and passenger, sustained injuries in a collision between their car and the defendant's. They were not wearing seat belts.

HELD: it was for the defendant to show that if the plaintiffs had been wearing seat belts they would have been less severely injured. He had not discharged the onus. *Obiter*, the law does not require a driver in Mr. Smith's position on a one way flyover driving absolutely normally to foresee that a madman would drive up the flyover in the wrong direction at high speed; the idea that the insurers of a grossly negligent driver should be relieved in any degree from what is proper compensation for the injuries because the occupants were not wearing seat belts is an idea which offends ordinary decency.

Smith v. Blackburn,
[1974] 2 Lloyd's Rep. 229 (O'Connor, J.)

The plaintiff was a passenger in the defendant's car when it left the road and hit a post. She was not wearing the seat belt fitted in the car though she knew of the advisability of wearing one; she found difficulty in fixing it and did not bother. The defendant was not wearing one and to the plaintiff's knowledge had been driving for 13 years without accident,

PAGE

185 The evidence showed that if the plaintiff had been wearing a seat belt
cont. some of her injuries would have been avoided.

HELD: the plaintiff was not guilty of contributory negligence. No one could have foreseen that the vehicle would be driven off the road into a post. The chance that an accident will occur in any individual case is extremely remote. Most people go through their whole lives without being involved in an accident. Dicta of Shaw, J., in CHALLONER V. WILLIAMS and O'Connor, J., in SMITH V. BLACKBURN (above) followed.

Chapman v. Ward,
[1975] 1 Lloyd's Rep. 309 (Stocker, J.)

The plaintiff was a passenger in the defendant's car when he sustained injury in an accident (facts on p. A11 above). Neither of them was wearing a seat belt.

HELD: there is a duty on a driver to bring to the notice of the passenger that there is a seat belt and that if he does not wear it he should accept the consequences. In this case neither of them gave it a thought; the defendant could not allege contributory negligence on the part of the plaintiff.

James v. Parsons,
[1975] 1 Lloyd's Rep. 178 (Kilner Brown, J.)

"I cannot resist remarking that judges who have expressed the opposite view [that it is negligent not to wear a seat belt] might reflect whether they have ever worn a seat belt in the back of the car which brings them to court . . . I have never seen a judge suggest that the driver of his car should wear the seat belt provided for him, neither have I seen such a driver wear it. Counsel has never seen a London taxi driver wear a seat belt. Neither have I . . . I do not think it undesirable for me to say that, looking as an ordinary mortal at the drivers of cars, the vast majority do not wear seat belts. Must this court say that the unfortunate plaintiff, having forgotten to put on the seat belt, was negligent because she failed to do that which so many others do not do? I think not and I will not". (Sir George Baker, P.)

Freeborn v. Thomas,
[1975] R.T.R. 16

Froom v. Butcher

A head-on collision occurred, wholly by the negligence of the defendant, between his car and a car driven by the plaintiff. The injuries sustained by the plaintiff included an abrasion of the scalp, fracture of the fourth right rib and fracture of a bone in the right hand. He was not wearing the seat-belt fitted in the car for his use. He said he did not like wearing one and had heard of cases where belts had caused danger. The judge held on the medical evidence that the injuries might had been slighter if the belt had been worn; the issue was whether the driver's omission to wear the belt constituted negligence or lack of care. There were two bodies of opinion of which the dominant opinion was that belts should be worn.

PAGE

185 *cont.* Nevertheless proper respect should be paid to the minority view; the courts were not justified in invading the freedom of choice of a motorist by holding it to be negligence or lack of care or fault to act on an opinion firmly and honestly held and shared by many other sensible people. The plaintiff's damages should not be reduced ([1974] R.T.R. 528).

HELD ON APPEAL: the judge's view was not right. In determining responsibility the law took no notice of the views of the particular individual. It required everyone to exercise all such precautions as a man of ordinary prudence would observe. As it is compulsory for every motor car to be fitted with seat belts Parliament must have thought it sensible to wear them. The material before the court about the value of wearing a seat belt showed plainly that everyone in the front seats of a car should wear one. The Highway Code advised wearing them. Wearing them only when there was a high risk as on a motorway in a fog was not enough; every time a car went out on the road there was a risk of accident. Forgetfulness was no excuse but there might be exceptional cases where a person might be excused from wearing a belt—for example, an unduly fat man or pregnant women. Apart from such cases a person failing to wear a seat belt should accept some share of responsibility for the damage if it could have been prevented or lessened by wearing one. The question how much the share should be should not be prolonged by an expensive enquiry into the degree of blameworthiness. If the injuries would have been prevented altogether by wearing a seat belt the reduction should be 25%. If the evidence merely showed that the injuries would have been a good deal less by wearing a belt damages should be reduced by 15%. In the present case 20% would be right. In the case of passengers a driver might have a duty to invite his passenger to fasten the seat belt but adult passengers should know they ought to wear a seat belt without being told.

Froom v. Butcher,
[1975] 3 All E.R. 520; [1975] 3 W.L.R. 379; 119 S.J. 613 (C.A.)

185 Road Traffic Act 1960, s. 117

In sub-s. (3) a "greater sum" of 11 new pence has now been prescribed by the Public Services Vehicles (Definition of Express Carriage) Regulations 1971, S.I. 1971 No. 1142, reg. 3.

188 Road Traffic Act 1972, s. 148(3)

Line 4: insert "agreement" after "antecedent" in copies where the word has been omitted.

199 After Moore v. Maxwells add.—

The plaintiff's car developed an electrical fault and as a result came to a stop at night by the nearside verge (to which the plaintiff had steered it) of a well-lighted road which was a clearway. There were no lights on the car; he took the battery to a garage on the other side of the road for recharging. Twenty minutes later the defendant driving his car at about 30 miles an hour did not see the plaintiff's car in time and crashed into the back of it. The County Court judge held the plaintiff wholly to blame: he said the plaintiff had not discharged the onus of proof placed on him by Denning, L.J.'s ruling in HILL-VENNING V. BESZANT (quoted in main volume, p. 198).

HELD, ON APPEAL: the plaintiff was negligent in failing to borrow a red lamp from the garage to put by his car and perhaps (as the County Court judge held) for failing earlier to see the warning red light on the dash-

PAGE

199 board and failing to push the car on to the verge; but the defendant was
cont. also to blame for not seeing the plaintiff's car in time to pull up. The proper proportions of blame were 50–50. *Per* Buckley, L.J:. I do not think normal experience leads one to the conclusion that it is safe to assume that no one will ever park in a part of the roadway which is classified as a "Clearway", and it is incumbent upon every user of such a roadway to drive in a way which enables him to meet an emergency or hazard presented by the fact that someone has parked—it may be for unavoidable reasons, such as a breakdown—in the "Clearway".

Lee v. Lever,
[1974] R.T.R. 35 (C.A.)

200 **After Barber v. B.R.S. add.—**

On the M1 motorway at night an articulated lorry driven by Allen got out of control and came to a stop in a position blocking the middle and fast lanes. A car collided with it in the centre lane and remained there with rear lights on. Another lorry stopped in the nearside lane short of Allen's lorry with its headlights on to illuminate the stationary vehicles. Squires then came along driving his employers' lorry; he saw the vehicles ahead when 400 yards away but did not realise two lanes were obstructed. At 150 yards away he saw the vehicle in the nearside lane, braked and moved into the centre lane. He then realised that lane was also blocked; he applied the brakes harder, went into a skid and hit the lorry on the nearside, killing the plaintiff's husband who was standing in front of it. The judge held Squires wholly to blame; the fact that Allen caused an obstruction was not, bearing in mind the circumstances, a factor which contributed to the fatal accident.

HELD, ON APPEAL: there was no break in the chain of causation between the negligent driving of Allen and the death of the plaintiff's husband. If a driver so negligently manages his vehicle as to obstruct the highway and constitute a danger to other road users including those who are driving too fast or not keeping a proper look-out (but not those who deliberately or recklessly drive into an obstruction as in DYMOND V. PEARCE (main volume, p. 288)) then the first driver's negligence may be held to have contributed to the causation of an accident of which the immediate cause was the negligent driving of a vehicle which collided with it. Where a party guilty of prior negligence has created a dangerous situation which is still continuing to a substantial degree at the time of the accident which would not have happened but for the continuing danger he is responsible as well as the party subsequently negligent. HARVEY V. ROAD HAULAGE EXECUTIVE (main volume, p. 199) and BARBER V. BRITISH ROAD SERVICES (main volume, p. 200) followed. Allen held 25% to blame.

Rouse v. Squires,
[1973] Q.B. 889; [1973] 2 All E.R. 903; [1973] 2 W.L.R. 925; 117 S.J. 431 (C.A.)

202 **After Drew v. Western S.M.T. Co. add.—**

The defendant was driving his car on a fast, wide road at night when the engine stopped and he came to a standstill by the nearside verge but not on it. He then attempted to re-start the engine by operating the self-starter. The plaintiff driving his van in the nearside lane from the same direction at 45–50 m.p.h. saw the two rear lights of the defendant's car

PAGE

202 when he was about 400 yards away and they then seemed to him to dis-
cont. appear. He thought the car must have turned off on to a slip road. He did not see it again until he was quite close. He applied his brakes heavily but struck the car, pushing it 57 feet. The judge concluded that the apparent disappearance of the car's rear lights was due to the defendant's use of the self-starter, causing the lights to dim or go out and that the defendant was 60% to blame.

HELD: on the defendant's appeal, the judge was entitled to find as he did.

Young v. Chester,
[1974] R.T.R. 70 (C.A.)

221 **Motor Vehicle (Construction and Use) Regulations 1969**

Revoked and replaced as from February 13, 1973 by the Motor Vehicles (Construction and Use) Regulations 1973 (S.I. 1973 No. 24).

Regulations 93, 96, 97 and 98 in the 1969 regulations have become regs. 112, 115, 116 and 117 in the 1973 regulations, and 117 has become reg. 137.

223 **Badham v. Lambs**

The equivalents in the 1973 Construction and Use Regulations for regs. 39 and 68 of the 1947 regulations are regs. 59 and 90.

224 **Motor Vehicles (Tests) Regulations 1960**

Revoked and replaced as from November 11, 1968 by the Motor Vehicles (Test) Regulations 1968 (S.I. 1968 No. 1714). Regulation 13 of 1960 is replaced by reg. 14 of 1968.

225 **After Rowley v. Chatham add.—**

On December 13, 1967, the plaintiff delivered his car to the defendants, who were authorised examiners for the annual M.O.T. test. After the test they issued a notification of refusal of a certificate saying that the nearside front hub bearing needed renewal. The plaintiff obtained a new bearing and the defendants fitted it. Without further test they then issued a test certificate on December 14. Five weeks later during which the plaintiff had driven the car 700 miles it suddenly veered across a busy main road and collided with an approaching vehicle, injuring the plaintiff. It was found that steering joints were loose. The plaintiff sued the defendants for damages for personal injury.

HELD: following ROWLEY'S case (main volume, p. 225) there is a duty on an examiner in contract to carry out the test properly and with reasonable skill and care and the issue of a test certificate bearing the prescribed wording also imports a warranty that the statutory requirements prescribed by the regulations were complied with at the date of the examination; (2) though a claim for damages either in contract or tort may be difficult to establish because of the lapse of time there is no reason in principle (contrary to the view expressed in ROWLEY'S case) why substantial (as distinct from nominal) damages should not be recovered by a plaintiff who can prove a failure to carry out the examination with proper skill and care and the issue of a test certificate which should not have been issued and that loss and damage were thereby caused; (3) if a plaintiff himself was guilty of some degree of carelessness in driving at the time of the accident the court can make an apportionment as between the causative faults under the Law Reform (Contributory Negligence) Act 1945 even if the claim is regarded as lying solely in contract; (4) on the

PAGE

225 *cont.* facts of the present case the plaintiff had failed to prove any breach of contract or duty in relation to the brakes or steering. Action dismissed.

Artingstoll v. Hewen's Garages, Ltd.,
[1973] R.T.R. 197 (Kerr, J.)

257 **After Burnside v. Emerson add.—**

The plaintiff was badly injured when a car in which she was a passenger on a narrow lane at night swung across the road and collided with an approaching vehicle. The lane was commonly used as a secondary traffic route but the highway authority had done no repair work for at least six months. The edges of the tarmac had broken away in places causing gaps where the nearside wheels of vehicles would pass; the judge accepted that the driver's loss of control was due to this state of disrepair. He held the highway authority two-thirds to blame.

HELD: dismissing the highway authority's appeal, the judge was right. They had failed to perform their statutory duty under s. 44 of the Highways Act 1959 to keep the highway in repair. They had further failed to discharge the duty implied in s. 1(2) of the Highways (Miscellaneous Provisions) Act 1961 to maintain the road in such a way as to secure that there was no danger for traffic. Whether part of the highway is a danger for traffic is a question of fact to be decided in a common sense way; but it was not correct that the test of danger is the risk to a careful driver. The duty of maintaining the highway free of danger is owed to all users who use the highway in the way normally to be expected of them—including some who may be rated as negligent. In the present case a finding of one-third negligence on the part of the car driver was justified on the ground that, with knowledge of the state of the lane he should have been going more slowly.

Rider v. Rider,
[1973] Q.B. 505; [1973] 1 All E.R. 294; [1973] 2 W.L.R. 190; 117 S.J. 71 (C.A.)

262 **After Bright v. Attorney General add.—**

Note: in RIDER V. RIDER (above,) members of the Court of Appeal disagreed with the final sentence of the passage from Lord Denning's judgment in BRIGHT's case; they did not accept as a matter of law that a danger for traffic cannot exist unless the road conditions constituting it would be a trap for the careful driver. Highway authorities must not provide only for those who use reasonable care.

265 **Penny v. Wimbledon Urban Council**

Highways Act 1959, s. 190 repealed by Local Government Act 1972.

288 **Under heading "Builder's skip on roadway" add.—**

King was driving his car in the hours of darkness along a residential road with the plaintiff as passenger when he collided with a builder's skip which he did not see in time to avoid. The skip had been placed partly on the grass verge and partly on the roadway by the owners who had delivered it on the instructions of the hirers. The hirers were builders doing work on a nearby house. They arranged for the house-owner, their customer, to put a lamp at each offside corner of the skip. Two motorists passing the skip 2 to 3 hours before the accident had seen the skip only just in time to swerve and avoid it.

PAGE

288 HELD: the provision of two lamps which so many persons failed to see
cont. was not adequate lighting. An object like a skip was very dangerous unless proper warning was given by lighting which would be readily and instantly apparent: this skip in its position and condition was a nuisance in the highway. The fact that King failed to see it was not fatal to his claim, but driving at a reasonable speed and being alert as a driver should at night he should have seen it. He was 40% to blame. The builders were liable as having taken detailed charge of the safety precautions. The owners of the skip were equally to blame with the builders having put the obstruction in the carriageway and left it there; they were under a duty to light it and could not escape liability by delegating the duty to someone else. The house-owner was not liable; he had merely done what he was asked to do.

Saper v. Hungate Builders, Ltd.,
[1972] R.T.R. 380 (Cantley, J.)

Note: in DYMOND V. PEARCE (main volume, p. 288) Sachs, L.J., considered there were two categories of nuisance: either an obstruction which was not dangerous, or one which was. Edmund Davies, L.J., in the same case thought an obstruction in a highway did not become a nuisance unless it was shown to be dangerous. This difference of view was alluded to in the following two cases:—

[Replace Wills v. T. F. Martin (Roof Contractors), Ltd. by the following]:

Riding a moped in the hours of darkness along a residential road which was poorly lit the plaintiff collided with a skip which he had not seen. It was on the nearside of the roadway and the plaintiff said it was unlighted. He was injured and claimed damages in nuisance and negligence against the roofing contractors who had put it there.

HELD: applying DYMOND V. PEARCE (main volume, p. 288), you have first to consider whether the presence of the skip on the highway is a nuisance. If the plaintiff satisfies that burden he has still to show, according to Edmund Davies, L.J. (in DYMOND's case), that the obstruction was also a dangerous obstruction. The last link in the chain is that the plaintiff must satisfy the court that the obstruction was at least a cause of the accident. A skip placed on a highway is in a different category from a parked vehicle. It has no business to be on the highway at all; to deposit a container of that character on the highway creates a nuisance. The skip was a nuisance because it was occupying a section of the highway which ought not to be obstructed in that way. If unlit in this position on the road it would be potentially dangerous, but on the evidence it was not established that it was unlighted. The sole cause of the accident was the plaintiff's failure to look where he was going and the claim failed.

Wills v. T. F. Martin (Roof Contractors), Ltd.,
[1972] R.T.R. 368 (Forbes, J.)

The defendant Council had placed a skip against the nearside kerb of a one-way street 35 feet wide. It was six feet wide and of much the same colour as the road surface and unlighted: the street lighting was adequate but not good. The plaintiff riding a scooter in the early morning before it was light failed to see the skip in time and collided with it.

HELD: as a matter of law, adopting Sachs, L.J.'s view in DYMOND's case, the skip was an obstruction and as such constituted a nuisance; it did not

PAGE

288 matter either that it occupied only 6 feet of a 35 foot-wide road, nor that
cont. the street lighting was or was not good. If the view of Edmund Davies, L.J. in DYMOND's case was correct, and in any event on the alternative claim in negligence, it was necessary to decide further whether the obstruction was dangerous. On the facts and the evidence it was. The final question was one of causation: did the presence of the skip play any causative part in the occurrence of the accident or was the plaintiff's failure to keep a proper look-out the sole cause? Bearing in mind all the circumstances, the nature of the road, the lighting and the amount of traffic which had avoided the skip, the existence of the nuisance did play a part but the plaintiff was 50% to blame in failing to keep as good a lookout as he should.

Drury v. Camden Borough Council,
[1972] R.T.R. 391 (May, J.)

308 **After B.G. Transport Service v. Marston Motor Co. add.—**

See also JAMES BUCHANAN CO., LTD. V. HAY'S TRANSPORT SERVICES, LTD., [1972] 2 Lloyd's Rep. 535.

321 **After Gillespie v. Bowles add.—**

The decision was reversed on appeal. If the words of the clause were sufficient to show an express agreement to indemnify the carriers even against claims arising from the negligence of their own servant, effect must be given to them. The use of the word "whatsoever" in the phrase "all claims or demands whatsoever" signified an intention that the indemnity was to extend to all claims of whatsoever kind without exception. The first of the requirements propounded in CANADA STEAMSHIP LINES V. R. (main volume, p. 317) was satisfied and it was unnecessary in this case to apply the second and third.

Gillespie Brothers, Ltd. v. Roy Bowles, Ltd.,
[1973] Q.B. 400; [1973] 1 All E.R. 193; [1973] 3 W.L.R. 1003; 116 S.J. 861 (C.A.)

357 **After Home Office v. Dorset Yacht Co., Ltd. add.—**

See also ROBINSON V. POST OFFICE, below, p. A33.

360 **After S.C.M. (U.K.), Ltd. v. W. J. Whittall & Son, Ltd. add.—**

The plaintiff's factory was supplied with electricity by a direct cable from the power station. The defendants were doing work in a road about a quarter-mile from the factory and negligently damaged the cable causing the power supply to the factory to be cut off for 14 hours. As a result the plaintiffs suffered loss from (1) damage to metal in an electric furnace; (2) loss of profit on that melt of metal; (3) loss of profit on metal which they would have subsequently melted during the period the power was off.

HELD: the plaintiffs were entitled to damages under heads (1) and (2) but not head (3). The loss under head (3) was economic loss independent of the physical damage to the metal in the furnace when the power failed.

Spartan Steel and Alloys, Ltd. v. Martin & Co. (Contractors), Ltd.,
[1973] Q.B. 27; [1972] 3 All E.R. 557; [1972] 3 W.L.R. 502; 116 S.J. 648 (C.A.)

PAGE

360 **After British Westinghouse Co. v. Underground Electric Co. add.—**

The plaintiff was a driving school proprietor. In 1967 he was negotiating to instal an electronic simulator to teach driving but because of injuries he had sustained in an accident for which the defendant was responsible the negotiations broke down. A simulator would have cost him £1824 a year for five years and then £71 per year. In 1971 he was able to, and did, buy one outright secondhand from a company in liquidation. But for this purchase his net loss of profit on simulator teaching would be £2774; if the defendant was entitled to take the purchase of the secondhand simulator into account the loss was nil. It was argued for the plaintiff that sums which came to him as a result of the tortious act and would not have come to him but for the tort were not to be taken into account.

HELD: the plaintiff had a duty to mitigate his damage by buying equipment just as much when that damage arose in tort as if it had arisen in contract. Applying the principles set out by Lord Haldane in BRITISH WESTINGHOUSE V. UNDERGROUND ELECTRIC RAILWAYS CO. (above) the damages were to be arrived at by subtracting the profits the business earned after the wrong had been suffered from the profits the business would have earned on the hypothesis that the defendant's wrong had not reduced them, looking at the whole of the facts and ascertaining the result. On this basis no loss arose on the simulator venture.

Bellingham v. Dhillon,

[1973] Q.B. 304; [1973] 1 All E.R. 20; [1972] 3 W.L.R. 730; 116 S.J. 566 (Forbes, J.)

362 **After Watson Norie Ltd. v. Shaw add.—**

On November 27 the plaintiff's taxi was damaged. He obtained an estimate of the cost of repair on December 1 and claimed the estimated amount from the defendant. He did not instruct the repairers to carry out the repairs, not being able to afford them and believing he had to allow the defendant's insurers to inspect the vehicle and also to get permission from his own insurers. It was not until January 26 that the defendant's insurers wrote agreeing the cost of repairs after an engineer's inspection. The plaintiff then instructed the repairers and the repairs were completed by February 25. Meanwhile the plaintiff had hired a replacement vehicle for ten weeks, starting a month after the accident. The defendant contested payment of the hire charges on the ground that the repairs should have been put in hand immediately after the accident.

HELD: it was not a case like THE LIESBOSCH. The plaintiff was seeking to recover his damages from the defendant's insurers and, if that went wrong, to recover from his own insurers. Until he had authorisation to do the work he could not be certain of being in a good position vis-à-vis the insurance company.

Martindale v. Duncan,

[1973] 2 All E.R. 355; [1973] 1 W.L.R. 574; 117 S.J. 168 (C.A.)

364 **After note following Darbishire v. Warren add.—**

Repairs causing loss of value

The plaintiff's car, only four weeks old, was damaged by the defendant. He claimed from her not only the cost of repairs but also the sum of £100

PAGE

364 being the estimated loss of market value of the car, even after repair, due
cont. to its being a repaired car. The judge awarded only the cost of repairs, finding on the evidence that no diminution in market value had been established by the plaintiff.

HELD, ON APPEAL: the judge's finding of fact must be accepted, but *obiter*, if the judge had found that the diminution in value had been established the plaintiff would have been entitled to an award. The normal measure of damages is the cost of repair but if, despite good repairs, a reduced market value can be proved, compensation for the reduction can be awarded to the plaintiff, the value of his property as a saleable asset having been reduced.

Payton v. Brooks,
[1974] R.T.R. 169 (C.A.)

364 **After note following Moss v. Christchurch R.D.C. add.—**

The defendants' lorry crashed into a row of three ancient cottages owned by the plaintiff company, causing damage. Two of the cottages were occupied as an office and store by the plaintiffs; the third was occupied by a statutory tenant at a rent of 15 shillings per week and was so badly damaged that she had to move elsewhere, losing her tenancy. The plaintiffs claimed the estimated cost of reinstating all the damaged cottages at a cost of £4079. At the trial it appeared that the plaintiffs, even before the accident, had intended to demolish the cottages and build new premises in place of them; the departure of the tenant had now enabled them to do this, for which they had obtained planning permission.

HELD: a claim for damage to property was either for cost of reinstatement or diminution in value. The evidence showed that the plaintiffs had no intention of reinstating; the departure of the statutory tenant had increased the value rather than diminished it. The only damages the plaintiffs were entitled to was the cost of a temporary repair already done and an agreed sum for loss of rent.

Hole & Sons, Ltd. v. Harrisons,
[1973] 1 Lloyd's Rep. 345 (Q.B.D.)

379 **After Povey v. Jackson add.—**

The plaintiff was awarded £48,682 damages for personal injuries. She appealed against the amount awarded. The defendant sought to defend the award on the ground that though items of the award might be too low, the global figure was consonant with other awards, citing POVEY v. JACKSON.

Per Sachs, L.J.: Whatever may have been the differing judicial views up to a few years ago and indeed up to 1970 as to whether a judge should simply award a global sum or whether he should state in his judgment what are the main components in that figure, the modern practice . . . is to adopt the second course . . . [The] plaintiff and defendant alike are entitled to know what is the sum assessed for each relevant head of damage and thus be able on appeal to challenge any error in the assessments. . . . It is of course always open to a respondent to do something which was not done here; that is, to give a cross-notice [of appeal] that even if one head as awarded by the judge is held to be demonstrably too low, some other head is demonstrably too high and thus seek to produce what is sometimes called a swings and roundabouts position. In other circumstances it

PAGE

379 *cont.* seems to me that a court should normally be slow to deal with an appeal on such a basis.

George v. Pinnock,
[1973] 1 All E.R. 926; [1973] 1 W.L.R. 118; 117 S.J. 73 (C.A.)

380 **After Fletcher v. Autocar and Transporters, Ltd. add.—**

The plaintiff was 14 when injured in a road accident. The main damage was to her brain: though she had been able after the accident to complete her education and pass GCE examinations she would not be able to take up a career nor do ordinary domestic tasks, such as cooking. She would probably never marry. She was of good middle-class background and might, but for the injuries, have become a solicitor or civil servant. The judge awarded her £20,000 for loss of future earnings (15 years at £1500 p.a.); and £15,974 for the cost of a housekeeper when she would need a place to live of her own.

HELD: on the defendants' appeal (1) the award of £20,000 for loss of amenities for life was justified; (2) £22,500 for loss of future earnings was too much. She might have married and not have been able to earn so much; damages for loss of marriage prospects were already compensated for in the first item; in any event she might not have earned for any great length of time. (3) on the third item there was doubt whether she would in fact set up in a flat of her own; having regard to the uncertain prospect and the amounts awarded for the other items the right figure for cost of future support was £6000. It was very important where a judge was following the modern practice of sub-dividing the claim under various headings to avoid overlapping. There was here a serious overlap between the allowance made for loss of the plaintiff's prospects of marriage on the one hand and loss of future earnings and the additional cost of domestic assistance on the other.

Harris v. Harris,
[1973] 1 Lloyd's Rep. 445 (C.A.)

382 **After Cutts v. Chumley add.—**

The plaintiff was a girl of 19 injured in a road accident (see p. A7 above). As a result she suffered from spastic quadriplegia. Her memory was grossly impaired, she could stand only with difficulty, could not do her hair or fasten buttons, could only partly dress herself and needed help for bath and lavatory. Her speech was scarcely intelligible; though damaged intellectually she was keenly aware of her pitiful condition. The judge awarded her £41,412 of which £1262 was special damage, £3150 future loss and £37,000 general damages. The defendant appealed, claiming that £37,000 was out of proportion to awards in similar cases—e.g. WEST V. SHEPHARD (main volume, p. 450).

HELD: the award should stand. The figure of £37,000 covered everything not covered by the other heads of damage, including nursing care in the event of the death or exhaustion of the plaintiff's mother as well as the plaintiff's loss of marriage prospects and thereby the support of a husband. There was a combination of crippling handicaps with a painful awareness of how much she had lost.

Powell v. Phillips,
[1972] 3 All E.R. 864; 116 S.J. 713 (C.A.)

PAGE
387 **After Mulholland v. Mitchell add.—**

McCann was badly injured in a motor accident in August 1968. The injuries were to the lower part of his body, impairing his urinary and sexual functions; there was permanent wasting and weakness of the right leg; he was permanently disabled from work. In June 1970 he married and though his sex life was practically nil his wife had a baby in September 1971. Because of great pain from his injuries McCann needed a pain-killing drug, palfrium. By the date of the trial of his action for damages in June 1972 he had become reliant on the drug. He was awarded general damages for pain, suffering and loss of amenities of £20,000, £15,000 for loss of future earnings (15 years at £1000 per year) and special damage of £2548. The defendants lodged notice of appeal in July 1972. On October 18 McCann was convicted in the magistrates' court of procuring drugs by deception. On October 22, 1972, he was found dead from an overdose of drugs. The hearing of the defendants' appeal was begun on February 28, 1973.

HELD: by the Court of Appeal (1) evidence of McCann's death should be admitted. Where notice of appeal has been served within the time prescribed by the rules and an event has taken place at a time reasonably proximate to the date of the trial which falsifies the facts on which judgment proceeded the Court of Appeal should not rehear the matter on the basis of the fiction that the event has not taken place; (2) damages for future loss of earnings must consequently be reduced from 15 years at £1000 per year to 20 weeks at £20 per week; (3) though his death had reduced the period during which McCann suffered pain and disability to four years the pain had been great; the award for that item should be £15,000; (4) £750 should be awarded for loss of expectation of life.

McCann v. Sheppard,
[1973] 2 All E.R. 88; [1973] 1 W.L.R. 540; 117 S.J. 323 (C.A.)

389 **After Liffen v. Watson add.—**

CARE AND NURSING

The plaintiff became tetraplegic as a result of a road accident. His mother, brother and two lodgers in his mother's house looked after him. His mother waived the £4 per week she had formerly received from the lodgers in consideration of their help. His brother took a job at a lower wage so as to have more time to look after him. Later the plaintiff entered into written contracts to pay his mother £12·60 per week and his brother £10 a week to look after him.

HELD: the plaintiff could not claim in his action for damages the £4 per week his mother had waived nor his brother's loss of wages since he was under no legal liability to make good that loss, but he was under a legal liability to pay the amounts he had contracted to pay them and it was reasonable to assess future nursing expenses at £22·60 per week.

Hagger v. de Placido,
[1972] 2 All E.R. 1029; [1972] 1 W.L.R. 716; 116 S.J. 396 (May, J.)
See next case.

The plaintiff, aged six, received injury to his leg in a road accident. After his discharge from hospital his mother gave up her work for six

PAGE

389 months to look after him. The judge awarded the plaintiff £147 in
cont. respect of her loss of earnings. On appeal the defendant argued that the item was not claimable by the plaintiff but that his mother might have recovered it had she been a party to the action.

HELD, ON APPEAL: the loss of the mother's wages was rightly claimed by and awarded to the plaintiff. It was his own loss—the existence of the need for nursing services of his mother, valued for the purposes of damages as the proper and reasonable cost of supplying those needs. It does not matter, so far as concerns the defendant, how or by whom the services have been provided nor whether the plaintiff has a legal liability to repay the provider. Nor is the existence of a moral obligation a material factor, nor an agreement between the injured person and the provider of the services to pay for them. On this point HAGGAR V. DE PLACIDO (above) was wrong. ROACH V. YATES, [1938] 1 K.B. 256 was authority for holding that the plaintiff was entitled to recover damages referable to the past and future financial value of voluntary services rendered to a plaintiff by others. LIFFEN V. WATSON (main volume, p. 389) embodied the same principle. Contrary to the defendant's "concession" the plaintiff's mother would not have been entitled to recover the loss herself had she been a party.

Donnelly v. Joyce,

[1974] Q.B. 454; [1973] 3 All E.R. 475; [1973] 3 W.L.R. 514; 117 S.J. 488 (C.A.)

The plaintiff's neck was broken in a motor accident, paralysing him for life in all four limbs and his body. He was entirely dependent on others for dressing, bath, evacuation of bowels and feeding. His wife did everything for him for two years, then committed suicide. Trial of his action for damages came three days afterwards. The judge awarded £18,000 for pain and suffering and loss of amenities, £18,050 ($9\frac{1}{2} \times$ £1900) for future loss of earnings and £33,250 ($9\frac{1}{2} \times$ £3500) for future cost of nursing and attendance. The judge accepted 12 years as an estimate of future expectation of life. Because of a difficult personality the plaintiff was considered unsuitable to enter a home and would have to live and be looked after in his own home.

HELD, ON APPEAL: (1) the figure of £18,000 for pain and suffering was right; (2) a voluntary *ex gratia* payment of £828 a year which the plaintiff's employers were making him and would continue to make for life was not to be taken into account; (3) on the evidence the multiplicand at £1900 a year for loss of earnings was right but the multiplier should be seven, since the plaintiff was 50 and would have retired at 60; (4) had the plaintiff's wife continued to look after him the value of her nursing services could have been claimed by the plaintiff without his having to make an agreement with her to pay her for them. On recovering such damages he would hold them on trust for her and pay them over to her; (5) the judge's award for the cost of future nursing was too high. There should be moderation in all things, even in a claim for personal injuries. It was not right that the defendant should have to pay extra because of the plaintiff's difficult personality. Moreover it would be difficult to find people to look after him at home all the time and he would sometimes have to use other and state-provided facilities e.g. under

PAGE
389 the Chronically Sick and Disabled Persons Act 1970. £2600 a year was
cont. an appropriate annual figure for provision of future nursing; the judge's multiplier of 9½ was about right on a life expectation of 12 years; (6) judges should not be required to make prophecies about the future rate of inflation.

Cunningham v. Harrison,
[1973] Q.B. 942; [1973] 3 All E.R. 463; [1973] 3 W.L.R. 97; 117 S.J. 547 (C.A.)

The plaintiff was 3½ when injured, 9 at the date of trial. Very serious head injuries left him unable to control his limbs properly, unable to walk, unable to speak properly, permanently unemployable. The judge awarded £27,500 for pain and suffering and disability, £18,000 for future nursing and care and £16,000 for potential loss of earnings. With some agreed items the total was £63,000.

HELD, ON APPEAL: both on the individual items and looked at in the round the award should stand. On particular points, (1) the item for care and nursing should not be any less if the plaintiff is looked after at home instead of in an institution. It is now settled that compensation can be given in money for services rendered by parents; (2) the fact that at the plaintiff's age calculation of future loss of earnings is extremely speculative is no ground for awarding merely a nominal sum. The present practice is to calculate a likely figure for future loss on present rates of earnings and having regard to the plaintiff's family background.

Taylor v. Bristol Omnibus Co.,
[1975] 2 All E.R. 1107; [1975] 1 W.L.R. 1054; 119 S.J. 476 (C.A.)

The plaintiff became a quadriplegic as a result of a diving accident. He was completely bedridden and everything had to be done for him by his wife who nursed him with outstanding care and devotion.

HELD: (*per* Lord Denning), in CUNNINGHAM V. HARRISON (above) I ventured to say that an award of damages could be made for a wife's services in nursing her injured husband. Even though she had not theretofore been doing paid work, but only domestic duties in the house, nevertheless all extra attendance on him called for compensation. It is not necessary for her to enter into a legal agreement as if she was a paid nurse. Sufficient that she had rendered services which would otherwise have had to be paid for. But I do not think that the award should be as high as that required for outside help. The wife does, after all, fit this extra work into her ordinary household duties and does it out of her wifely duty to keep him in sickness and in health. It is difficult to suggest an appropriate figure but I would suggest £15 a week or £780 a year . . . His expected life is 10 years from the trial. The present value of this may be taken at £780 multiplied by seven.

Davies v. Tenby Corporation,
[1974] 2 Lloyd's Rep. 469 (C.A.)

406 **After Jones v. Griffiths add.—**

See also STEPHENSON V. COOK, [1975] 1 Lloyd's Rep. 495.

PAGE

407–8 **Road Traffic Act 1972, s. 156**

Amended by the National Health Reorganisation Act 1973: in sub-s. (1)(a) the words from "National Health Service Act 1946" to the end are replaced by "National Health Service Acts 1946 to 1973, to the Area Health Authority or special health authority responsible for the administration of the hospital or to the Secretary of State if no such authority is responsible". Paragraphs (b) and (c) of sub-s. (1) are repealed.

410 **After British Transport Commission v. Gourley add.—**

The defendant was awarded £495 damages on a counterclaim for wrongful dismissal, less tax to be decided by the Court. The defendant had earned £1343 in the tax year, on which he had paid tax of £23. If he had earned the additional £495 as income he would have paid a total of £160 in tax. The plaintiffs contended that the damages of £495 should be reduced by £137 being the additional tax that would have been attracted by £495 treated as the top slice of his income. The defendant claimed that only the average rate of tax between the £495 and the other income should be deducted.

HELD: the plaintiffs' contention was right. The principle in GOURLEY's case (main volume, p. 410) plainly applied. If a comparison was to be made between a given income and that income with something added, the addition must be treated as the top part of the income; it was the increase in the income which attracted the higher rates of tax.

Lyndale Fashion Manufacturers v. Rich,
[1973] 1 All E.R. 33; [1973] 1 W.L.R. 73; 117 S.J. 54 (C.A.)

The plaintiff was off work for 19 weeks as a result of injury and claimed loss of earnings for that period calculated on the weekly pre-accident wage after deduction of income tax on a PAYE basis. Afterwards he received a tax rebate of £81·70 due to his not having earned wages during the 19 weeks off work.

HELD: applying the principles of GOURLEY's case, his claimed loss should be reduced by the amount of the tax rebate. The saving of tax to the plaintiff was not too remote but stemmed directly from the consequences of the accident; it was not *res inter alios acta* nor completely collateral, and the amount of the saving was not a matter of speculation but was accurately quantified.

Hartley v. Sandholme Iron Co., Ltd.,
[1975] Q.B. 600; [1974] 3 All E.R. 475; [1974] 3 W.L.R. 445; 118 S.J. 702 (Nield, J.)

413 **After Stedman v. Swans Tours add.—**

The plaintiff booked a holiday with the defendants for himself, his wife and their three-year-old twin sons in Ceylon for a month at a cost of £1450. For the first fortnight they were housed in a hotel which did not fulfil the description given in the defendants' brochure. The judge awarded £1100 damages for (a) the difference in value between what the plaintiff got and what he bargained for; (b) compensation for distress and disappointment.

HELD, ON APPEAL: the award should stand. The plaintiff was making

PAGE

413 a contract for the benefit of the whole family. He could recover damages
cont. for the discomfort, vexation and upset which the whole family suffered.

Jackson v. Horizon Holidays, Ltd.
The Times, Feb. 6, 1974 (C.A.)

At end of note headed "Special Damage" add.—

See also cases under heading "Care and Nursing" above, pp. A28, A30.

419 **After Rose v. Ford add.—**

"The judge held that when a man is aware of his loss of expectation of life the damages should be increased so as to take his awareness into account. I quite agree. Such damage does not come in as part of the conventional award for 'loss of expectation of life'. It comes in as part of the damages for 'pain and suffering and loss of amenities'." (*Per* Lord Denning.)

Davies v. Tenby Corporation,
[1974] 2 Lloyd's Rep. 469 (C.A.)

422 **N.H.S. (General Medical and Pharmaceutical Services) Regs.**

The 1966 regulations (S.I. 1966 No. 1210) were revoked and replaced by S.I. 1972 No. 1602 which themselves have been replaced by the N.H.S. (General Medical and Pharmaceutical Services) Regulations 1974 (S.I. 1974 No. 160).

423 **National Health Service (Amendment) Act 1969, s. 28**

The National Health Service Reorganisation Act 1973 deletes the words "hospital and specialist services" and substitutes "services under the National Health Service Acts 1946 to 1973".

429 **After McAuley v. London Transport Executive add.—**

"The plaintiff in the present case is not in the slightest degree a malingerer and is a completely honest man who genuinely holds the beliefs about which he has told us in evidence. But in deciding whether the defendants have proved that he had unreasonably refused to have the investigation and operation in question here, it seems to me clear from the authorities to which I have referred [STEEL V. ROBERT GEORGE & CO., (main volume, p. 430) MARCROFT V. SCRUTTONS, LTD. (main volume, p. 429)] that I must apply an objective test, in this sense, would a reasonable man, in all the circumstances, receiving the advice the plaintiff did receive, have refused the operation? I think this question must be considered as at the times when his decision was made and on the basis of the advice he then received. If the plaintiff preferred and prefers to go on as he is rather than have the operation [for removal of a prolapsed intervertebral disc] no one can blame him. But the question I have to consider is not, 'Is the plaintiff to blame for refusing the operation?' but 'Is it fair and reasonable to make the defendants pay for his refusal?'" (*per* Browne, J.).

Morgan v. T. Wallis, Ltd.,
[1974] 1 Lloyd's Rep. 165 (Q.B.D.)

430 **After Hogan v. Bentinck Collieries, Ltd. add.—**

The plaintiff, a Post Office employee, sustained a wound on his leg when he slipped on an oily rung whilst descending a tower wagon ladder. He visited his doctor who gave him an injection of anti-tetanus serum.

PAGE

430 *cont.* A few days later the plaintiff developed symptions due to an allergy to the serum and eventually suffered serious brain damage. The judge held that the doctor was not negligent in administering the serum and that although he was negligent in failing to give a preliminary test dose it would have made no difference if he had. The Post Office admitted that accident and injury to the plaintiff's leg were caused by negligence on its part but said it was not liable for the serious results of the injection because they were not reasonably foreseeable.

HELD: (1) the injection of serum by the doctor was not a *novus actus interveniens* which broke the chain of causation between the negligence of the Post Office and the plaintiff's disability caused by the injection. Conduct of the doctor falling short of negligence could not amount to a *novus actus* and such negligence as the judge found against him was of no effect in causing the disability; (2) it was foreseeable both that the plaintiff might slip on an oily rung and sustain injury and that if he did he might well require medical treatment. The only unforeseeable result was the terrible extent of the injury caused by the plaintiff's allergy to the serum; in that respect the Post Office must take their victim as they found him. SMITH V. LEECH BRAIN & CO. (main volume, p. 346) followed. If a wrongdoer ought reasonably to foresee that as a result of his wrongful act the victim may require medical treatment he is, subject to the principle of *novus actus interveniens*, liable for the consequences of the treatment applied although he could not reasonably foresee those consequences.

Robinson v. Post Office,
[1974] 2 All E.R. 737; [1974] 1 W.L.R. 1176; 117 S.J. 915 (C.A.)

439 After note following Mulvaine v. Joseph add.—

See also TAYLOR V. BRISTOL OMNIBUS CO. (above, p. A30).

450 After Andrews v. Freeborough add.—

A child a year old sustained brain damage in the course of a surgical operation. Thereafter he was blind and deaf and did not react to stimuli of light, heat, sound, cold, hunger, comfort and discomfort. He died aged 3 years 10 months. Damages for loss of amenity were assessed at £5000 and loss of expectation of life at £500.

Gray v. Mid Herts Group Hospital Management Committee,
(1974), 118 S.J. 501 (Waller, J.)

451 Law Reform (Personal Injuries) Act 1948

In sub-s. (1) the words "or invalidity" were inserted after the word "sickness" by the National Insurance Act 1971. Sub-s. (1) is now further amended by the Social Security (Consequential Provisions) Act 1975 by replacing the words from "industrial injury" to "invalidity benefit" by the following.—

"any of the following benefits under the Social Security Act 1975 or the Social Security (Northern Ireland) Act 1975, namely—

sickness benefit
invalidity benefit
non-contributory invalidity pension
injury benefit
disablement benefit".

For sub-s. (6) of s. 2 the following was substituted by the Social Security

PAGE

451 *cont.* Act 1973 and now (the 1973 Act having been repealed) by the Social Security (Consequential Provisions) Act 1975, Sch. 2.—

"(6) for the purposes of this section disablement benefit in the form of a gratuity is to be treated as benefit for the period taken into account by the assessment of the extent of the disablement in respect of which it is payable".

452–453 **National Insurance Acts**

The National Insurance Act 1965 and the National Insurance (Industrial Injuries) Act 1965 were repealed as from April 6, 1975 by the Social Security (Consequential Provisions) Act 1975. For s. 2(6) of the Law Reform (Personal Injuries) Act 1948 see above. Section 5 of the National Insurance (Industrial Injuries) Act 1965 is reproduced in s. 50 of the Social Security Act 1975 except that "industrial injury benefit" and "industrial disablement benefit" are called respectively "injury benefit" and "disablement benefit". Section 7 of the 1965 Act reappears as s. 52 of the 1975 Act. Section 8 of the 1965 Act is reproduced as s. 53 of the 1975 Act except that "insured person" becomes "employed earner", and "hovercraft" is added after "vessel" in sub-s. (2).

453 **"To be taken into account"**

See now the amendment to s. 2(1) of the Law Reform (Personal Injuries) Act 1948 set out above, p. A33.

457–459 **Rates of benefit**

The rates set out in the text are no longer effective. The number and frequency of the increases in social security benefits makes it impracticable to maintain an up-to-date list of rates in this work. Sections 3 and 4 of the Social Security Benefits Act 1975 (already repealed and replaced by similar provisions in ss. 124 and 125 of the Social Security Act 1975) give the Secretary of State both a power and a duty to up-rate benefits to keep pace, in effect, with the general level of earnings and prices. Details of the current rates of benefit can be obtained from the offices of the Department of Health and Social Security.

463 **Fatal Accidents Act 1846**

In s. 3 the words "and that every" to the end of the section are repealed by the Limitation Act 1975.

465 **After Fatal Accidents Act 1959, s. 1 add.—**

The plaintiff claimed damages under the Fatal Accidents Acts for the death of her husband. She was the second wife of the deceased, whose first marriage was dissolved in 1967 and custody of the children of that marriage was awarded to the first wife. In the present action the first (i.e former) wife applied to the Court to be joined as a dependant in the widow's action.

HELD: the former wife was not a dependant within the meaning of the Fatal Accidents Acts. Neither s. 2 of the 1846 Act nor s. 5 of the 1959 Act in defining the class of dependants made any provision which included a divorced husband or wife as a person on whose behalf an action could be brought.

Payne-Collins v. Taylor Woodrow Construction, Ltd.,
[1975] Q.B. 300; [1975] 1 All E.R. 898; [1975] 2 W.L.R. 386; 119 S.J. 49 (O'Connor, J.)

PAGE

467 **After Bradburn v. G.W.R. Co. add.—**

The first plaintiff's husband, a successful businessman, had over the years made various dispositions of his money for her benefit and that of their son. He was killed in a road accident by negligence of the defendant's driver before the period of seven years had elapsed; as a result nearly £40,000 was brought back for estate duty and £17,000 duty was paid.

HELD: in the claim by the widow and son under the Fatal Accidents Acts, the sum of £17,000 (less £500 to cover the small chance of the deceased's not surviving the remainder of the seven years had the accident not happened) was recoverable from the defendants as damages for the death. It (1) was a financial loss which the plaintiffs had suffered and would suffer as a result of the death and (2) arose from the relationship of husband and father, and was accordingly within the words of s. 2 of the 1846 Act.

Davies v. Whiteways Cyder Co., Ltd.,
[1974] Ch. 186; [1974] 3 All E.R. 168; [1974] 2 W.L.R. 333; 118 S.J. 100 (O'Connor, J.)

474 **After Taylor v. O'Connor add.—**

The deceased, aged 29 at the time of his death, was employed as a sales representative by a travel firm. His annual income net of tax was £1615 and the dependency of the plaintiff widow and their two children was £1100. Evidence was given of likely increases in the deceased's earnings. Some of the increases would result from promotion and some would be given to meet the rising cost of living.

HELD: (1) the multiplier of the figure for dependency at death, i.e. £1100, should be 14 having regard to all the factors—the ages of the deceased and the plaintiff (both approaching 30), the fact that the deceased had not long been in the job and that it was in a trade of uncertain profitability; (2) by the date of trial, 3½ years after his death, the dependency would probably, but not certainly, have increased to £2100 per annum on salary increases resulting from promotion. The multiplier for this increased dependency of £1000 per annum should, because of the imponderable factors, be eight years only; (3) following TAYLOR V. O'CONNOR (main volume, p. 474) the estimates or forecasts given in evidence of future earnings increases referable solely to anticipations of future inflation must be excluded from the assessment.

Young v. Percival,
[1974] 3 All E.R. 677; [1974] 1 W.L.R. 17; 119 S.J. 33 (C.A.)

474 **Fatal Accidents Act 1959, s. 2**

In sub-s. (2) in the definition of "benefit" the words from "National Insurance" to "Parliament of" are replaced by the words "enactments relating to national insurance and social security including enactment in force in" by the Social Security Act 1973, Sch. 27, para. 20.

474 **After note following Fatal Accidents Act 1959, s. 2 add.—**

The deceased was killed a month before his sixtieth birthday when he would have received a lump sum from his employers. Had he then worked to sixty-five he would have received another lump sum and a pension. His widow had now received from the employers a lump sum and a

PAGE

474 widow's pension. If these were to be disregarded in assessing damages
cont. because of the provisions of s. 2 of the Fatal Accidents Act 1959 she would be better off than if her husband had survived. It was argued for the defendants that she had first to prove pecuniary loss to claim damages under the 1846 Act and if because of the benefits she had received she had no loss the 1959 Act did not apply.

HELD: that was not right. The wording of s. 2(1) of the 1959 Act was very clear: the benefits to the widow by reason of her husband's death were to be disregarded in deciding whether or not there had been a loss and what should be the damages by way of compensation.

Humphrey v. Ward Engineering Services, Ltd.
(1975), 119 S.J. 461 (Latey, J.)

476 **After Davies v. Powell Duffryn Associated Collieries add.—**

In an action carried on under the 1934 Act the administrators of the estate of J. M. Murray claimed damages for injuries and loss of earnings he sustained as a result of a road accident in January 1969. He remained in a coma until he died in April 1973 (see main volume, p. 421). After his death the administrators began an action under the Fatal Accidents Acts on behalf of his widow and children. The actions were consolidated. In the first action the net damages awarded for injuries and loss of amenities were £7837 and for loss of earnings £4613. In the F.A.A. action the provisional figure for damages was £76,800. The question to be decided was by how much, if any, the gross damages in the F.A.A. action should be reduced by deducting damages awarded to the estate in the first action.

HELD: (1) as the sum of £7837 awarded to the estate for loss of amenities would pass to the widow and children as beneficiaries under the intestacy the provisional F.A.A. damages should be reduced by that amount; (2) deduction of the loss of earnings was different: had Mr. Murray earned that amount he would have used it for their benefit in his lifetime. It would be unjust to reduce the compensation paid to the dependants for loss of his support after his death because of the belated receipt of money which, but for the defendant's wrongdoing, would have been used for their financial support in the four years or so preceding his death. None of it should be regarded as deductible.

Murray v. Shuter,
[1975] 3 All E.R. 375; [1975] 3 W.L.R. 597; 119 Sol. Jo. 712 (C.A.)

481 **Davies v. Taylor; substitute the following:—**

The plaintiff and her husband were married in 1955. From December 1966 to February 1968, unknown to her husband she had an adulterous association with a man she met at work. In May 1968 she gave up her job and on the 9th July she left her husband saying she no longer had any feeling for him. She went to live with her parents. Her husband very much wanted her to return to him and begged her to do so. On July 31 he went to her and asked her to return but she told him of her adulterous affair. On the 2nd August he instructed solicitors to begin divorce proceedings. On August 14 he met the plaintiff by chance, in the street, told her he had consulted a solicitor but again asked her to return to him; she refused, saying she wanted time to think. Later on the same day he was killed in a motor accident. At the trial of the plaintiff's claim for

PAGE

481 *cont.* damages under the Fatal Accidents Acts the judge said that on the question of dependency the test he had to apply was whether the plaintiff had discharged the onus of proving that it was more probable than not that there would have been a reconciliation between her and her husband. He said he was not satisfied there was likely to be a reconciliation and that accordingly the plaintiff had not proved any dependency.

HELD: the judge had applied the wrong test. In this case it had to be decided whether there was a reasonable expectation of a reconciliation, not whether a reconciliation was more likely than not. If, although there was a reasonable expectation, the chance of the reconciliation happening was slight then the damages would be such as would reflect that degree of probability. The plaintiff's damages would be scaled down as the possibility became progressively more remote. But a mere speculative or fanciful possibility of a reconciliation was not sufficient. On the evidence the judge had rightly decided that there was no likelihood of a reconciliation and the plaintiff's claim failed. TAFF VALE RLY. CO. V. JENKINS (main volume, p. 482) applied.

Davies v. Taylor,
[1974] Q.B. 207; [1972] 3 All E.R. 836; [1972] 3 W.L.R. 801; 116 S.J. 864 (H.L.)

481 **After note following Montgomery v. Blows add.—**

Savings

The plaintiff and her husband, both aged 19, were married in 1971. A child was born in November; in December the husband was killed. During the three months or so since marriage they had lived with his parents, paying £6 for accommodation. The husband had been earning £30 per week net of which they had put aside £10 per week in a bank account in her name alone. On an appeal against an award of £16,848 made by the judge using an agreed multiplier of 18, the defendants complained that the judge had made no reduction for the £10 weekly savings in determining the widow's dependency at £18 per week.

HELD: if the £10 per week had been spent instead of saved the standard of living of both spouses would have gone up. Some part of the £10 per week, whether saved or spent, should be regarded as likely to have been spent eventually for the benefit of the husband himself. To that extent the loss was not the widow's. The dependency should be reduced by £3 per week to £15.

Gavin v. Wilmot Breedon, Ltd.,
[1973] 3 All E.R. 935; [1973] 1 W.L.R. 1117; [1973] 2 Lloyd's Rep. 501 (C.A.)

482 **After note following Read v. G.E.R. Co. add.—**

In MCCANN V. SHEPPARD (see p. A28) the question was raised whether in the events which happened in that case, the plaintiff's widow could have a cause of action under the Fatal Accidents Acts. Lord Denning and James, L.J., were of the opinion that the wording of s. 1 of the act "would appear to put an insuperable obstacle in the path of such proceedings".

486 **After Rawlinson v. Babcock and Wilcox, Ltd. add.—**

Mr. and Mrs. Hay, aged 29 and 25, were killed in a road accident. Their children, aged 4½ and 2½, were then taken by their maternal

PAGE

486 grandmother, Mrs. Toone, into her own home and cared for by her.
cont. She did so without thought of being paid and intended to continue to bring them up. Mr. Hay was a welder at the time of his death who would, at the date of trial, have been earning £40 per week. Mrs. Hay did not work. In assessing damages for the children under the Fatal Accidents Acts the judge adopted a figure of £1100 per annum as the amount by which they were worse off by the loss of their father and £1000 per annum by the loss of their mother. The latter figure was based on the assumed cost of providing a housekeeper or nanny. He took a multiplier of 8 and, after deducting £2500 representing the value of the parents' estates, awarded £16,400 damages. On appeal it was argued for the defendant (1) the replacement of the deceased's mother's services not having taken place no award for the pecuniary loss of those services should be made; (2) the services rendered by Mrs. Toone in looking after the children for nothing were "benefits resulting from the death" and should be taken into account.

HELD: the award was right. On (1) the fact that a widower decided to manage for himself after the death of his wife would not disentitle him to sue for and recover damages for the pecuniary loss he had nevertheless sustained. Similarly the fact that the orphaned children had not incurred the expense of a housekeeper did not destroy or diminish their right to be compensated. On (2) it is not possible to discover from the decided cases any established principle to determine whether the benefits conferred by Mrs. Toone on the children should be taken into account or not. It was a jury question to which the judge addressed himself and decided in a way which seemed fair, namely, that Mrs. Toone's care conferred no benefit which should be taken into account. The principle that the assessed loss of a plaintiff should be reduced by any pecuniary advantage coming to him by reason of the death has been so seriously eroded by legislation that in the light of history the court should hesitate to extend the principle to classes of benefit not directly covered by binding authority.

Hay v Hughes,

[1975] 1 All E. R. 257; [1975] 2 W.L.R. 34; [1975] 1 Lloyd's Rep. 12 (C.A.)

489 **After Phipps v. Cunard White Star add.—**

The plaintiffs sued under the Fatal Accidents Acts for damages for the three children of a self-employed labourer, killed in an accident. The deceased and the unmarried mother of the three children had lived as man and wife for a number of years and their children at his death were aged 6, 5 and 3. The mother continued to look after the children, drawing supplementary allowance of £10·40 per week for herself and £8·70 for them. The deceased's earnings had been about £2800 per annum. In addition to usual living expenses he had paid for holidays in Ireland, toys for the children and family outings. The judge awarded damages on the basis that the children were entitled to awards which would enable the mother to provide the same standard of living as the deceased had provided, that is, including the cost of the mother's upkeep: he assessed the children's loss at a figure which included all the deceased's expenditure other than that on himself. The judge applied the number of years' purchase from the date of the trial to 16 years of age for each child. The defendants appealed.

PAGE

489 cont. HELD: (1) as the mother was now receiving supplementary allowance for herself the amount awarded to the children in respect of her share of upkeep and benefits from the deceased's income should be reduced by the amount of her necessary living expenses paid for by her supplementary allowance; (2) contrary to the contention of counsel for the children the mother would not lose her entitlement to supplementary benefit by reason of the aggregation of the damages awarded to the children since she would not be "a person [who] has to provide for the requirements of another person" within the meaning of Sch. 2 of the Social Security Act 1966 when the children's needs were provided for by the awards of damages; (3) the judge was not in error in fixing 16 as the age at which the children would have ceased to be dependent on the deceased but the years of purchase should have been calculated from the date of death, not from the date of trial. Awards increased to £3836 for eldest child, £4384 for middle child and £5480 for the youngest.

K. v. J.M.P. Co., Ltd.,
[1975] 1 All E.R. 1030; [1975] 2 W.L.R. 457; 119 S.J. 188 (C.A.)

493 **After Reincke v. Gray add.—**

As s. 4(1) applies to damages "payable to a widow" the proportion of damages allotted to a child is to be assessed, where the widow had remarried, having regard to that fact.

Deceased 24 years old at death, widow 22, child 18 months. Widow remarried 2 years 3 months later, the second husband being in as good a financial position as the deceased would have been. Dependency of widow £9 per week, multiplier 17 years having regard to ages of deceased and widow. Child entitled to 2 years 3 months at £3 per week (£337·50) rounded up to £500 to allow for his receiving perhaps less from step-father than he would from his own and having to compete with children of second marriage.

Thompson v. Price,
[1973] Q.B. 838; [1973] 2 All E.R. 846; [1973] 2 W.L.R. 1037; 117 S.J. 468 (Boreham, J.)

508 **After Cain v. Wilcock add.—**

The deceased was a youth aged 17. Actuarial evidence was given (July 1972) that the pound sterling had depreciated 40% in value since 1966.

HELD: general damages for loss of expectation of life £700; the time had come for the conventional figure of £500 to be increased.

King v. Jodrell,
[1972] 7 C.L. 120 (Hollings, J.)

In MCCANN V. SHEPPARD (above, p. A28) the Court of Appeal awarded £750 for loss of expectation of life without mentioning earlier decisions.

511 **Administration of Estates Act 1925, s. 46**

In the case of deaths after July 1, 1972 the fixed net sum for the spouse is £15,000 in place of £8,750 where the deceased leaves issue and £40,000 in place of £30,000 where there is no issue. (Family Provision (Intestate Succession) Order 1972, S.I. 1972 No. 916).

PAGE

517 **The Limitation Acts**

In place of the *Summary* substitute the following: Actions founded on tort or on simple contract must be brought within six years of the accrual of the cause of action (Limitation Act 1939, s. 2), except in the case of claims for damages for personal injury due to negligence, nuisance or breach of duty; the special rules relating to such claims are set out in the Limitation Act 1975, below. An action is "brought" when the writ or summons is issued whether or not it is served. Time does not run against a person under disability whilst the disability lasts (Limitation Act 1939, s. 22). In cases of negligence the cause of action accrues when the damage is caused, subject to the special provisions in the Limitation Act 1975 in cases of personal injury and death. The Limitation Act 1963 provides a time limit of two years for bringing proceedings to recover contribution from another tortfeasor. A defendant who wishes to rely on a statute of limitations must plead it (see R.S.C., O. 18, r. 8(1)).

Limitation Act 1939

The proviso to s. 2(1)(a) is repealed by the Limitation Act 1975, which by s. 1 inserts four new sections, numbered 2A to 2D, into the Limitation Act 1939 as follows:—

2A.—(1) This section applies to any action for damage for negligence, nuisance or breach of duty (whether the duty exists by virtue of a contract or of provision made by or under a statute or independently of any contract or any such provision) where the damages claimed by the plaintiff for the negligence, nuisance or breach of duty consist of or include damages in respect of personal injuries to the plaintiff or any other person.

(2) Section 2 of this Act shall not apply to an action to which this section applies.

(3) Subject to section 2D below, an action to which this section applies shall not be brought after the expiration of the period specified in subsections (4) and (5) below.

(4) Except where subsection (5) applies, the said period is three years from—

(*a*) the date on which the cause of action accrued, or

(*b*) the date (if later) of the plaintiff's knowledge.

(5) If the person injured dies before the expiration of the period in subsection (4) above, the period as respects the cause of action surviving for the benefit of the estate of the deceased by virtue of section 1 of the Law Reform (Miscellaneous Provisions) Act 1934 shall be three years from—

(*a*) the date of death, or

(*b*) the date of the personal representative's knowledge.

whichever is the later.

(6) In this section, and in section 2B below, references to a person's date of knowledge are references to the date on which he first had knowledge of the following facts—

(*a*) that the injury in question was significant, and

(*b*) that that injury was attributable in whole or in part to the act or omission which is alleged to constitute negligence, nuisance or breach of duty, and

(*c*) the identity of the defendant, and

(*d*) if it is alleged that the act or omission was that of a person other than the defendant, the identity of that person and the additional facts supporting the bringing of an action against the defendant,

and knowledge that any acts or omissions did or did not, as a matter of law, involve negligence, nuisance or breach of duty is irrelevant.

(7) For the purposes of this section an injury is significant if the plaintiff would reasonably have considered it sufficiently serious to justify his instituting proceedings for damages against a defendant who did not dispute liability and was able to satisfy a judgment.

PAGE
517 (8) For the purposes of the said sections a person's knowledge includes know-
cont. ledge which he might reasonably have been expected to acquire—

(*a*) from facts observable or ascertainable by him, or
(*b*) from facts ascertainable by him with the help of medical or other appropriate expert advice which it is reasonable for him to seek,

but a person shall not be fixed under this subsection with knowledge of a fact ascertainable only with the help of expert advice so long as he has taken all reasonable steps to obtain (and, where appropriate, to act on) that advice.

(9) For the purposes of this section 'personal representative' includes any person who is or has been a personal representative of the deceased, including an executor who has not proved the will (whether or not he has renounced probate) but not anyone appointed only as a special personal representative in relation to settled land; and regard shall be had to any knowledge acquired by any such person while a personal representative or previously.

(10) If there is more than one personal representative, and their dates of knowledge are different, subsection (5)(*b*) above shall be read as referring to the earliest of those dates.

2B.—(1) This section has effect subject to section 2D below.

(2) An action under the Fatal Accidents Act 1846 shall not be brought if the death occurred when the person injured could no longer maintain an action and recover damages in respect of the injury (whether because of a time limit in this Act or in any other Act, or any other reason).

Where any such action by the injured person would have been barred by the time limit in section 2A above, no account shall be taken of the possibility of that time limit being overridden under section 2D of this Act.

(3) An action under the Fatal Accidents Act 1846 shall not be brought after the expiration of three years from—

(*a*) the date of death, or
(*b*) the date of knowledge of the person for whose benefit the action is brought,

whichever is the later.

(4) Subsection (3) above shall not apply to an action for which a period of limitation is prescribed by or under any Act other than this Act, and section 2A above shall not apply to an action under the Fatal Accidents Act 1846.

(5) An action under the Fatal Accidents Act 1846 shall be one to which section 22 of this Act (persons under disability) applies, but otherwise Part II and Part III of this Act shall not apply to the action.

2C.—(1) This section applies where there is more than one person for whose benefit an action under the Fatal Accidents Act 1846 is brought.

(2) Section 2B(3)(*b*) shall be applied separately to each of them, and if that would debar one or more of them, but not all, the court shall direct that any person who would be so debarred shall be excluded from those for whom the action is brought unless it is shown that if the action were brought exclusively for the benefit of that person it would not be defeated by a defence of limitation (whether in consequence of section 22 of this Act (persons under disability), or an agreement between the parties not to raise the defence, or otherwise).

2D.—(1) If it appears to the court that it would be equitable to allow an action to proceed having regard to the degree to which—

(*a*) the provisions of section 2A or 2B of this Act prejudice the plaintiff or any person whom he represents, and
(*b*) any decision of the court under this subsection would prejudice the defendant or any person whom he represents,

the court may direct that those provisions shall not apply to the action, or shall not apply to any specified cause of action to which the action relates.

(2) The court shall not under this section disapply section 2B(2) except where

PAGE
517 the reason why the person injured could no longer maintain an action was
cont. because of the time limit in section 2A.

If, for example, the person injured could at his death no longer maintain an action under the Fatal Accidents Act 1846 because of the time limit in Article 29 in Schedule 1 to the Carriage by Air Act 1961, the court has no power to direct that section 2B(2) shall not apply.

(3) In acting under this section the court shall have regard to all the circumstances of the case and in particular to—

(*a*) the length of, and the reasons for, the delay on the part of the plaintiff;
(*b*) the extent to which, having regard to the delay, the evidence adduced or likely to be adduced by the plaintiff or the defendant is or is likely to be less cogent than if the action had been brought within the time allowed by section 2A or as the case may be 2B;
(*c*) the conduct of the defendant after the cause of action arose, including the extent if any to which he responded to requests reasonably made by the plaintiff for information or inspection for the purpose of ascertaining facts which were or might be relevant to the plaintiff's cause of action against the defendant;
(*d*) the duration of any disability of the plaintiff arising after the date of the accrual of the cause of action;
(*e*) the extent to which the plaintiff acted promptly and reasonably once he knew whether or not the act or omission of the defendant, to which the injury was attributable, might be capable at that time of giving rise to an action for damages;
(*f*) the steps, if any, taken by the plaintiff to obtain medical, legal or other expert advice and the nature of any such advice he may have received.

(4) In a case where the person injured died when, because of section 2A, he could no longer maintain an action and recover damages in respect of the injury, the court shall have regard in particular to the length of, and the reasons for, the delay on the part of the deceased.

(5) In a case under subsection (4) above, or any other case where the time limit, or one of the time limits, depends on the date of knowledge of a person other than the plaintiff, subsection (3) above shall have effect with appropriate modifications, and shall have effect in particular as if references to the plaintiff included references to any person whose date of knowledge is or was relevant in determining the time limit.

(6) A direction by the court disapplying the provisions of section 2B(2) shall operate to disapply the provisions to the same effect in section 1 of the Fatal Accidents Act 1846.

(7) In this section "the court" means the court in which the action has been brought.

(8) References in this section to section 2A include references to that section as extended by any provision of Parts II and III of this Act."

The Limitation Act 1975 came into force on September 1, 1975, and in s. 3 contains the following transitional provisions:—

3.—(1) The provisions of this Act shall have effect in relation to causes of action which accrued before, as well as causes of action which accrue after, the commencement of this Act, and shall have effect in relation to any cause of action which accrued before the commencement of this Act notwithstanding that an action in respect thereof has been commenced and is pending at the commencement of this Act.

(2) For the purposes of this section an action shall not be taken to be pending at any time if a final order or judgment has been made or given therein, notwithstanding that an appeal is pending or that the time for appealing has not expired.

(3) It is hereby declared that a decision taken at any time by a court to grant,

PAGE

517 *cont.* or not to grant, leave under Part I of the Limitation Act 1963 (which, so far as it relates to leave, is repealed by this Act) does not affect the determination of any question in proceedings under this Act, but in such proceedings account may be taken of evidence admitted in proceedings under the said provisions repealed by this Act.

(4) In this section "action" includes any proceeding in a court of law, an arbitration and a claim by way of set-off or counterclaim.

518 **Limitation Act 1939, s. 22**

Sub-s. 2 (added by the Law Reform (Limitation of Actions etc.) Act 1954) is repealed by the Limitation Act 1975, of which s. 2 reads as follows:

2.—(1) At the end of section 22 of the Limitation Act 1939 (persons under disability: time limit of 6 years from end of disability) there shall be inserted the following subsections:—

"(2) If the action is one to which section 2A or 2B(3) of this Act applies subsection (1) of this section shall have effect as if for the words '6 years' there were substituted the words '3 years'.

(3) Where this section applies by virtue of section 4(3) of the Limitation Act 1963 (contribution between tortfeasors) subsection (1) of this section shall have effect as if for the words '6 years' there were substituted the words '2 years'".

(2) The provisions of this section are in substitution for the subsection (2) added to section 22 by the Law Reform (Limitation of Actions etc.) Act 1954, and in substitution for the proviso to section 4(3) of the Limitation Act 1963.

518 **Limitation Act 1939, s. 31**

The definition of "personal injuries" was added by s. 2 of the 1954 Act which is repealed by the Limitation Act 1975. Instead the following definition is substituted: "'personal injuries' includes any disease and any impairment of a person's physical or mental condition, and 'injury' and cognate expressions shall be construed accordingly" (Limitation Act 1975, Sch. 1, para. 3).

519 **After Limitation Act 1939 add.**—

The plaintiff instructed the defendants who were insurance brokers to obtain a policy covering the use of his motor lorry including passenger risks. The defendants omitted to ensure that the policy covered claims by passengers. The plaintiff was injured when riding as a passenger in his own lorry but was unable to recover damages from the driver because the policy did not cover him against passenger claims. More than three years but less than six years after the accident the plaintiff issued a writ against the defendants for failing to obtain passenger liability cover. They pleaded that the action was statute barred as being one where the damages claimed "consist of or include damages in respect of personal injuries to any person" (Limitation Act 1939, s. 2(1) as amended by the 1954 Act).

HELD: the action was not statute-barred. The question to ask was "What is the action all about?". The answer was that it was about an alleged breach of contract by the defendants whereby the plaintiff lost the right to recover his loss either from the driver or from his own insurers. The damages for personal injuries which he might have recovered

PAGE

519 were only the measure of the damages now claimed. The limitation
cont. period was thus six years not three.

Ackbar v. C. F. Green & Co.,

[1975] Q.B. 582; [1975] 2 All E.R. 65; [1975] 2 W.L.R. 773; 119 S.J. 219; [1975] 1 Lloyd's Rep. 673 (Croom-Johnson, J.)

Note: although the proviso to s. 2(1) of the Limitation Act 1939 added by the 1954 Act and containing the words "consist of or include damages in respect of personal injuries" has been repealed by the Limitation Act 1975 the same words appear in the new s. 2A inserted by that Act in the Limitation Act 1939 (above, p. A40).

Law Reform (Limitation of Actions &c.) Act 1954

Sections 2 and 3 are repealed by the Limitation Act 1975.

522 **After Kirby v. Leather add.—**

Note: s. 2 of the 1954 Act is repealed by the Limitation Act 1975. The protection of s. 22 of the 1939 Act is no longer denied to a person under a disability who is or was "in the custody of a parent".

523– **"In the custody of a parent"**
525 See note to KIRBY V. LEATHER above. For a final decision on the words see ROGERS V. EXETER AND MID-DEVON HOSPITAL MANAGEMENT COMMITTEE (1974), 119 S.J. 86.

525 **Limitation Act 1963**

Sections 1 to 3B inclusive are repealed by the Limitation Act 1975 together with s. 6 (transitional provisions) and all of s. 7 except part of sub-s. (7). The requirement to obtain leave of the Court to take proceedings disappears and the cases on applications for leave cease to be of any value. The words "material fact" and "facts of a decisive character" are not used in the Limitation Act 1975; it follows that the cases on the meanings to be attached to those words (main volume, pp. 527–530) give no help in interpreting the 1975 Act.

530 **Limitation Act 1963, s. 4**

The proviso to sub-s. 3 is repealed by the Limitation Act 1975. For the statutory provision replacing it see the Limitation Act 1975, s. 2(1) (above, p. A43).

534 **After note following Wimpey v. BOAC add.—**

Two banks sued a company and the chairman of the company for conversion in the same action. In the Court of first instance both defendants were found not liable. On appeal the company was found liable and judgment entered but a retrial was ordered of the action against the chairman. On retrial the judge found the chairman responsible for the conversion but held that the action against him was barred because of the final judgment already entered against the company. Section 6(1)(a) of the 1935 Act (as reproduced in the law of Singapore) removed the bar on a further action against a joint tortfeasor if he would "if sued, have been liable as a joint tortfeasor" and the chairman had already been "sued".

HELD: by the Privy Council, this was not right. "Liable" in the section means "held liable" and "if sued" means "if sued to judgment".

PAGE

534 *cont.* The judgment against the company was not a bar to judgment for conversion being entered against the chairman.

Wah Tat Bank, Ltd. v. Chan Cheng Kum,
[1975] 2 All E.R. 257; [1975] 2 W.L.R. 475; 119 S.J. 151 (P.C.)

545 **After Street v. Bebber add.—**

Accident August 18, 1969. Negotiations for settlement of claim started but became protracted by difficulty in getting instructions from the plaintiff. Writ issued August 17, 1972. In July 1973 defendants' insurers offered £3000. In September 1973, the writ not having been served and the plaintiff having refused the offer, the plaintiff's solicitors applied for renewal.

HELD: no renewal could be permitted. The fact that negotiations were in progress for a settlement at the time when the writ was about to expire was not a sufficient reason for not serving the writ.

Easy v. Universal Anchorage Co., Ltd.,
[1974] 2 All E.R. 1105; [1974] 1 W.L.R. 899; 118 S.J. 464 (C.A.)

549 **After Re Chittenden add.—**

By conduct of negotiations

Collision between two vessels August 28, 1969. Negotiations for settlement of claims begun between solicitors September 10, 1970 still continuing on July 2, 1971 when plaintiffs' solicitors issued writ and notified defendants' solicitors it was "to protect the two year time limit which would otherwise expire in August". Further discussions took place at long intervals. On August 3, 1972 the writ having expired and the latest offer from the defendants being still outstanding, the plaintiffs' solicitors applied ex parte for, and were granted, a renewal to August 27, 1972. The defendants applied for renewal to be set aside.

HELD: on the facts, there was an agreement that service of the plaintiffs' writ should be deferred so long as negotiations were continuing and the writ was rightly renewed. RE CHITTENDEN (main volume, p. 549) applied.

The Owenbawn,
[1973] 1 Lloyd's Rep. 56 (Brandon, J.)

550 **Add to preliminary note on Civil Evidence Act 1968.—**

The Civil Evidence Act 1972 makes hearsay statements of opinion admissible in evidence in civil proceedings to substantially the same extent as are hearsay statements of fact under the 1968 Act.

553 **After Ford v. Lewis add.—**

The defendants, sued for damages for injuries sustained by the plaintiff when knocked down by a bus, sought to put in evidence a written statement from a witness highly prejudicial to the plaintiff's case. The defendants served a notice on the plaintiff under R.S.C., O. 38, rr. 21 and 22(3) asserting that the witness could not be called because "She has left her former address number 225 Charles Road Small Heath Birmingham and cannot at present be found. It is understood that she is now beyond the seas and is probably resident in Jamaica". The defendants had made extensive enquiries in the Birmingham area to find the witness and had received information from two people that she had gone to Jamaica but they had made no enquiries in Jamaica to find her.

PAGE
553 The plaintiff served a counter-notice under r. 25(2) and claimed the
cont. defendants had not shown reasonable diligence in trying to find the witness.

HELD: (1) of the five reasons given in s. 8(2)(b) of the Civil Evidence Act 1968 the defendants' notice really invoked only the assertion that the witness could not be found, but the evidence of their enquiries was sufficient to show a probability that she was in fact beyond the seas; (2) the reasons given in s. 8(2)(b) are disjunctive: if the maker of the statement is beyond the seas it does not have to be proved also that she cannot by reasonable diligence be found; (3) if the Court is satisfied on any of the five specified reasons it has no residuary discretion to exclude the statement by reference to other circumstances; (4) though the defendants' notice was out of order it should have read simply "because she is beyond the seas". Order made accordingly.

Rasool v. West Midlands Transport Executive,
[1974] 3 All E.R. 638 (Finer, J.)

557 After Devine v. British Transport Commission add.—

Note: The Rules of the Supreme Court (Amendment) Order 1974 (S.I. 1974 No. 295) adds new rules numbered 36 and 37 to O. 38, requiring a party to an action to seek directions from the court before adducing expert evidence and dealing specifically with medical evidence as follows:—

Medical evidence in actions for personal injuries

37.—(1) Where in an action for personal injuries an application is made under rule 36(1) in respect of oral expert evidence relating to medical matters, then, unless the Court considers that there is sufficient reason for not doing so, it shall direct that the substance of the evidence be disclosed in the form of a written report or reports to such other parties and within such period as the Court may specify.

(2) The Court may, if it thinks fit, treat any of the following circumstances as a sufficient reason for not giving a direction under paragraph (1):—

(*a*) that the pleadings contain an allegation of a negligent act or omission in the course of medical treatment; or

(*b*) that the expert evidence may contain an expression of opinion—

(i) as to the manner in which the personal injuries were sustained; or

(ii) as to the genuineness of the symptoms of which complaint is made.

558 After Worrall v. Reich add.—

In the course of a claim against them for damages for personal injuries the defendants asked for medical examinations of the plaintiff and were granted them by the plaintiff's solicitors "on the usual terms" which was taken to mean merely on payment of the plaintiff's expenses. The plaintiff's solicitors obtained medical reports separately from time to time. The order for directions in the action ordered that a medical report be agreed upon if possible, and if not, medical evidence be limited to two witnesses for each party. The defendants' solicitors asked the plaintiff's solicitors for copies of all the reports they had obtained and were sent them. They then agreed the plaintiff's reports and refused to disclose their own. On the plaintiff's application for disclosure,

HELD: as was clear from WORRALL V. REICH (main volume, p. 558) a medical report was a privileged document and the Court had no power under O. 5, r. 6 to order its disclosure. There was nothing in the correspondence in the present case from which an agreement to exchange

PAGE

558 reports could be inferred, nor anything amounting to a waiver by the
cont. defendants of their privilege. The plaintiff's solicitors could have attached conditions to production of their reports but they did not. An agreement to disclose was not implied in the phrase "usual terms"; the plaintiff's solicitor should have told the defendants what agreement they were seeking or making so that no dispute could arise.

Causton v. Mann Egerton (Johnsons), Ltd.,
[1974] 1 All E.R. 453; [1974] 1 W.L.R. 162; [1974] 1 Lloyd's Rep. 197 (C.A.)

559 **After Mullard v. Ben Line Steamers add.—**

It is thoroughly undesirable, and indeed irregular, for the Court to be called upon to make its own choice between so-called agreed medical reports which are, in fact, in conflict . . . It is therefore well to sound a note of warning that the day may come when the Court, confronted with so-called agreed medical reports which in fact disagree with each other in a material respect, will have no alternative but to send the matter back for a further hearing (*Per* Edmund Davies, L.J.).

Hambridge v. Harrison,
[1973] 1 Lloyd's Rep. 572 (C.A.)

569 **In "Summary of High Court Action",** amend period for acceptance of payment into court from 14 days to 21 days.

594 **After Sayle v. Cooksey add.—**

Effect of delay before issue of writ

Cause of action (breach of contract) April 1963; Writ issued December 1967; pleadings closed December 1968; then no step by plaintiffs until notice of intention to proceed in February 1972.

HELD: inordinate and inexcusable delay after issue of writ but no prejudice to the defendants by this delay because their situation from the point of view of getting information had not deteriorated since about 1968. *Per* Buckley, L.J.: delay before the issue of the writ in an action or before the action once commenced ceases to be actively or timeously pursued, may have a bearing on whether delay which follows thereafter is to be regarded as inordinate and inexcusable but cannot itself be inordinate or inexcusable delay. If the facts are such that no additional prejudice to the defendant has arisen as the result of delay after the end of that period in which delay can be said to be excusable it cannot be right, in my judgment, for the court to dismiss the action.

William Parker, Ltd. v. Ham & Son, Ltd.,
[1972] 3 All E.R. 1051; [1972] 1 W.L.R. 1583; 116 S.J. 903 (C.A.)

But see following cases.

Plaintiff sustained injury on September 17, 1968. Writ issued August 10, 1971. No Statement of Claim. Defendants application to dismiss June 13, 1972.

HELD: action should be dismissed. The total delay from the accident must be looked at, not merely delay since issue of writ. WM. PARKER, LTD. V. HAM (above) dealt with special circumstances.

Mason v. F. A. Ashcroft (Cornmillers), Ltd.
(1973), 117 S.J. 449 (C.A.)

PAGE

594 Plaintiff injured on July 9, 1969. No claim made; writ issued on
cont. July 3, 1972 and served; no statement of claim. Defendants applied to strike out on April 3, 1973. Judge in chambers refused to strike out, holding that six months' delay after writ was not inordinate, and applying WM. PARKER LTD. V. HAM (above).

HELD, ON APPEAL: the action should be dismissed. As in MASON's case (above) the delay before issuing the writ should also be taken into account. WM. PARKER, LTD. V. HAM had no application to great majority of personal injury cases.

Sweeney v. Sir Robert McAlpine & Sons, Ltd.,
[1974] 1 All E. R. 474; [1974] 1 W.L.R. 200; [1974] 1 Lloyd's Rep. 128 (C.A.)

Accident February 3, 1968. Letter before action March 1968; denial of liability January 1969. Writ issued January 1971 served January 1972; Statement of Claim served February 1972. Medical Reports on possibility of epilepsy September 1971 and December 1972. June 1973 action dismissed for want of prosecution.

HELD, ON APPEAL: a fair trial was possible and the action should be allowed to go on. The delay had been inordinate and inexcusable but one had to look at all the circumstances and see whether one could have a fair trial. WM. PARKER, LTD. V. HAM had been said on two occasions to be a very special case and not of general application but (*per* Megaw, L.J.) it would not be right to say there was any conflict between that case and MASON's or SWEENEY's cases (above). The principles were laid down in ALLEN V. MCALPINE (main volume, pp. 587 and 588).

Kennedy v. Associated Electrical Industries, Ltd.
(1973), 118 S.J. 169 (C.A.)

Accident at school June 1965 when plaintiff was 13. Letter before action January 1967, writ issued April 1968, served May. Order to set down February 1972 but not done when action dismissed for want of prosecution March 1973.

HELD: dismissing the plaintiff's appeal, it was not right to say delay in the last year had made it only marginally worse. WM. PARKER, LTD. V. HAM (above) was a very special case on sale of goods with a 6-year limitation period and documentary material available. If the writ was issued within three years and served within four that was in a sense permissible but if that whole time was taken it was incumbent on the plaintiff to adhere to the Rules of Court thereafter and not cause any delay.

Briden v. Ashby
The Times, December 6, 1973 (C.A.)

595 **After Austin Securities v. Northgate add.—**

Writ issued October 7, 1969 claiming £1564 for hire of linen. After unsuccessful application for judgment under O. 14 plaintiffs took no further step. October 1971 on defendant's application action dismissed for want of prosecution, defendant saying on affidavit that he had been

PAGE

595 told claim had been abandoned. November 1971 plaintiffs issued new
cont. writ for £1564; defendant applied to strike out writ as an abuse of the Court.

HELD: the second action should be struck out. Though a new action could be started on the same cause of action it was always subject to the inherent jurisdiction to dismiss it as an abuse of the court. In the present case the plaintiffs had given no explanation for the new claim; it was an attempt to resurrect something that was dead and buried.

Spring Grove Services v. Deane
(1972), 116 S.J. 844 (C.A.)

The plaintiffs sued the defendant for £9000 arrears of National Insurance contributions by writ issued November 15, 1967. Nothing more was done until April 1972 when the plaintiffs gave notice of intention to proceed. On defendant's application the action was struck out for want of prosecution. Plaintiffs then issued a new writ on July 27, 1972 for the proportion of the £9000 not already statute-barred. Defendant applied to strike out second action as an abuse of the Court.

HELD: it should not be struck out. SPRING GROVE SERVICES V. DEANE did not mean that a second action would automatically be struck out. In that case there were good reasons for doing so. In the present case in which the defence was of the thinnest possible character and the defendant was not prejudiced in his defence there were not.

Department of Health and Social Security v. Ereira,
[1973] 3 All E.R. 421 (C.A.)

Note: in MAXWELL V. RAEBURN (1973), 117 S.J. 527 in the Chancery Division, where the facts were somewhat similar to EREIRA's case, the second action was likewise allowed to continue. No reference was apparently made to either SPRING GROVE SERVICES V. DEANE or EREIRA's case.

595 **After Kirkpatrick v. Salvation Army add.—**

Road accident July 1968. Letter before action June 1970, particulars of claim filed November 1970, defence three days later then action adjourned generally to allow defendant to join a third party. January 1971, leave to join third party then further adjournment. Hearing fixed by Court for June 1972, but further adjournment when third party died; his executors were joined November 1972. Court gave notice in June 1973 of intention to strike out unless hearing date applied for. Hearing fixed for August 9, 1973 but adjournment again applied for by parties' consent on August 2. On 9th judge struck it out of his own motion.

HELD: dismissing plaintiff's application for leave to appeal out of time from the judge's order, the delay had been quite shocking. In running down actions the memory of witnesses of matters which frequently happen in seconds deteriorates with the passing years. The rules of the Court are there to be observed and parties cannot by mutual cordiality agree to prolong the trial by agreeing to adjournments in the interlocutory stage. There is a supervising duty vested in the Court of scrutinising cases such as the present.

Kerr v. National Carriers, Ltd.,
[1974] 1 Lloyd's Rep. 365 (C.A.)

PAGE

598 **Crown Proceedings Act 1947, s. 17**

The list now in force was published in February 1973.

605 **After Burnell v. British Transport Commission add.—**

Discovery before proceedings

Section 31 of the Administration of Justice Act 1970 gives the Court power to order discovery and production of documents before proceedings against "a person who appears to the court to be likely to be a party to the proceedings" in which a claim in respect of personal injuries "is likely to be made".

A patient who entered hospital for investigations became gravely ill and her family suspected a wrong diagnosis and treatment. She obtained a legal aid certificate to get a medical opinion. She was examined by a specialist who said the hospital was probably not at fault but that his assessment of the medical aspect was considerably hampered by the absence of the hospital notes, and that he ought to see them. The hospital board refused to disclose them.

HELD: the claimant was entitled to an order for disclosure of the notes to the specialist. "Likely to be made" in the Act means "may well be made" dependent on the outcome of the discovery. The fact that the only basis for saying that a claim is not "likely" is the absence of the documents for which discovery is sought does not preclude the court from ordering their production; but the applicant must disclose the nature of the claim and show there is a reasonable basis for making it.

Dunning v. Liverpool Hospitals Board,
[1973] 2 All E.R. 454; [1973] 1 W.L.R. 586; 117 S.J. 167 (C.A.)

A factory worker was injured when a fork lift truck failed to stop, as it should, when he took his foot off the pedal. He applied to the Court for an order against his employers under s. 31 of the Administration of Justice Act 1970 for discovery of maintenance reports on the machine. The Judge in chambers refused an order, considering discovery should be made in the ordinary course of an action, if brought.

HELD: allowing the appeal, one of the objects of s. 31 is to enable a plaintiff to find out before he starts proceedings whether he has a good cause of action or not. That object would be defeated if he had to show in advance that he already had a good cause of action. He should set out the substance of his case in an open letter or other document which could if necessary be used at the subsequent trial, if any. An important aspect of the matter was that legal aid should not, in the public interest, continue beyond the point at which it is reasonably clear that the plaintiff has no prospect of success. Counsel in the present case had conceded that if the reports showed nothing wrong the applicant could not succeed in an action and litigation would be avoided.

Shaw v. Vauxhall Motors, Ltd.,
[1974] 2 All E.R. 1185; [1974] 1 W.L.R. 1035; 118 S.J. 347 (C.A.)

When an order is made under s. 31 against a hospital for production of the hospital notes and records to the plaintiff's medical adviser only,

PAGE
605 the plaintiff is not bound by his report but can write him for further advice
cont. or have him seen by counsel in conference as an expert witness.

Deistung v. S.W. Regional Hospital Board,
[1975] 1 All E.R. 573; [1975] 1 W.L.R. 213; 119 S.J. 13 (C.A.)

Discovery against a person not a party

Section 32 of the Administration of Justice Act 1970 gives the Court power in an action in respect of personal injuries to order a person who is not a party to the proceedings to disclose and produce documents which are in his possession, custody or power and which are relevant to an issue arising from the claim.

The plaintiff contracted a tropical disease on a journey to Tanzania made so urgently that there was no time for previous inoculations. Four years later he had severe heart trouble. In an action against his employers he applied for an order against a hospital for production of hospital notes preparatory to medical examination by a specialist in tropical diseases. The master made an order requiring production of the notes to the specialist only. The judge in chambers enlarged the order to include the plaintiff's solicitors.

HELD: on appeal by the hospital, the master's order was correct. The Winn committee (1968, Cmnd. 3691, para. 294) had recommended procedural provision for ensuring availability of hospital records at any medical examination. As a matter of principle discovery of medical notes and records should be confined in the early stages of an action at any rate to the medical men who have to examine and report. The notes may contain information or statements which would be embarrassing and distressing if made known to others. Cases do arise where to do justice it may be necessary to extend the discovery to solicitors or even to the party himself but this case was not one of them.

Davidson v. Lloyd Aircraft Services,
[1974] 3 All E.R. 1; [1974] 1 W.L.R. 1042; 118 S.J. 366 (C.A.)

615 **Following note under "Issue, trial of" add.—**

Cars driven by the plaintiff and defendant collided head-on, injuring both. The plaintiff, a German veterinary surgeon, claimed heavy damages including large sums for potential loss of earnings. Trial would be likely to be extended by four days by the evidence on damages. The defendant counter-claimed in respect of his own injuries and applied for separate trials on the issues of liability and damages. The Judge refused separate trials on the ground that the plaintiff was entitled to choose the normal method of trying liability and quantum at the same time.

HELD, ON APPEAL: this was not right. The Winn Committee had recommended a less restrictive approach to separate trials. Winn, L.J., himself had alluded to separate trials in HAWKINS's case. R.S.C., O. 33, r. 4(2) give the courts power to grant separate trials and they should be ready to do so wherever it is just and convenient. In the present case much time and expense in trying the issue of damages would be wasted if the plaintiff were to fail on the issue of liability. The plaintiff could not claim the right to choose merely by agreeing to pay for the extra expense. Appeal allowed.

Coenen v. Payne,
[1974] 2 All E.R. 1109; [1974] 1 W.L.R. 984; 118 S.J. 499 (C.A.)

PAGE

622 **After note at top of page add.—**

The second defendant asked for a medical examination of the plaintiff by two named doctors. The plaintiff agreed subject to her solicitors being supplied with copies of the reports. The second defendant objected to this requirement and applied for a stay until the plaintiff should grant facilities for the examination.

HELD: the plaintiff's stipulation was fair. It was reasonable and just as a condition of being granted a medical examination that the defendant should make available the doctor's report to the plaintiff. If and when the plaintiff got further reports on her own she must reciprocate and show those to the defendant.

Clarke v. Martlew,

[1973] 1 Q.B. 58; [1972] 3 All E.R. 764; [1972] 3 W.L.R. 653; 116 S.J. 618 (C.A.)

In an action for damages for personal injuries the defendant's solicitors asked permission to have the plaintiff medically examined. The plaintiff's solicitors stipulated that they must be supplied with a copy of the report. Defendant's solicitors were agreeable to this provided the plaintiff's solicitors supplied copies of all their own reports. They refused; the defendant's solicitors applied for a stay of the action.

HELD: the plaintiff must at least offer reciprocity. If the plaintiff's solicitors require to see a copy of the defendant's medical report immediately they must be prepared to offer an equivalent report of their own in exchange but they are not obliged to disclose all their reports. The Court is only concerned with those on which the plaintiff intends to rely at the trial. As an alternative to immediate disclosure the parties can agree to eventual exchange before trial.

McGinley v. Burke,

[1973] 2 All E.R. 1010; [1973] 1 W.L.R. 990; [1973] 2 Lloyd's Rep. 508.

632 **After Thornton v. Swan Hunter add.—**

Followed in BEAUMONT V. BRITISH URALITE, LTD. (1973), 117 S.J. 914.

645 **After Haigh v. Lawford add.—**

Cashing cheque

Some damage was done to the party wall between the plaintiff's and the first defendant's houses by contractors (the second defendants) employed by the first defendant. The plaintiff had the damage repaired and wrote the first defendant saying the repair had been done and that he would send him a copy of the account, adding "any further deterioration of my property . . . will result in a claim for compensation in addition . . ." Later he sent a copy of the account for the repairs at £18·15 "without prejudice to any further claim from the building work . . ." The second defendants sent the plaintiff a cheque for £18·15 "in full and final settlement of your claim against Mr. Galynski with regard to damage caused to the party wall". The plaintiff cashed the cheque.

PAGE

645 cont. HELD: he had compromised the matter and had no legal claim for any further compensation.

Bell v. Galynski and A. Kings Loft Extensions, Ltd.,
[1974] 2 Lloyd's Rep. 13 (C.A.)

646 After note following Trow v. Ind Coope add.—

The plaintiff's husband was killed at work on September 4, 1967. She issued a writ on September 7, 1970. September 5 and 6, 1970, were a Saturday and Sunday when the Court Office was closed for business.

HELD: (1) following MARREN V. DAWSON BENTLEY & CO., LTD. (main volume, p. 520) the day on which the cause of action arose was to be excluded from the computation of the three years limitation period; (2) when a time is prescribed by statute for doing any act which can only be done if the Court office is open on the day when the time expires then if that day is a Sunday or other *dies non* the time is extended to the next day on which the court office is open. Thus by issuing on September 7, 1970 the plaintiff was in time.

Pritam Kaur v. S. Russell & Sons,
[1973] Q.B. 336; [1973] 1 All E.R. 617; [1973] 2 W.L.R. 147; 117 S.J. 91 (C.A.)

653 Legal Aid

The Legal Aid and Advice Act 1949 has been repealed and replaced by the Legal Aid Act 1974 which, with minor exceptions, came into force on May 8, 1974.

653 After Starkey v. Railway Executive add.—

Section 1(7) of the 1949 Act is re-enacted in s. 2(5) of the 1974 Act.

654 After Law Society v. Rushman add.—

For s. 3(4) of the 1949 Act see now s. 9(6) of the 1974 Act.

654 After Anderson v. Hills Automobiles add.—

Section 2(2)(d) of the 1949 Act is re-enacted as s. 8(1)(d) of the 1974 Act.

655 After Nolan v. Marshall add.—

Section 4(3) of the 1949 Act is re-enacted as s. 11(3) of the 1974 Act.

656 After Carr v. Boxall add.—

Section 2(2)(e) of the 1949 Act is re-enacted as s. 8(1)(e) of the 1974 Act.

657 After Blatcher v. Heaysman add.—

Section 2(2) of the 1949 Act is re-enacted by s. 8(1) of the 1974 Act.

657 After Mercantile Credit Co. v. Cross add.—

See note to BLATCHER V. HEAYSMAN (above).

657 After Dugon v. Williamson add.—

See note to CARR V. BOXALL (above).

658 After Jackson v. John Dickinson add.—

Section 12(2)(b)(ii) of the 1949 Act is re-enacted as s. 20(2)(b)(ii) of the 1974 Act.

PAGE

658 Defendant's costs from Legal Aid Fund

The Legal Aid Act 1964 has been repealed and replaced as from May 8, 1974, by the Legal Aid Act 1974, ss. 13 and 14, without amendment.

661 After Saunders v. Anglia Building Society add.—

See also GENERAL ACCIDENT ASSURANCE, LTD. V. FOSTER, [1973] 1 Q.B. 50; [1972] 3 All E.R. 877; [1972] 3 W.L.R. 657; [1972] 2 Lloyd's Rep. 288.

SAUNDERS's case did not decide that an unassisted litigant who appeals to the Court of Appeal and wins is barred from recovering costs from the legal aid fund. He can recover his costs against the legal aid fund if it is just and equitable for him to do so, even though it was he who was the appellant. The fact that the unassisted party is of relatively limited means is a consideration that may be sufficient to justify an order.

Clifford v. Walker,
[1972] 2 All E.R. 806; [1972] 1 W.L.R. 724; 116 S.J. 275 (C.A.)

But see DAVIES V. TAYLOR (NO. 2), below, p. A55.

In the County Court both parties had legal aid, but in the Court of Appeal (see main volume, p. 853) the appellant Averay was unable to get legal aid and was supported by the Automobile Association whose solicitors acted for him. He applied under s. 1 (2) of the 1964 Act for his costs to be paid out of the legal aid fund.

HELD: an order should be made to that effect. Averay was the litigant and the costs were "incurred by him". It was just and equitable that he should have them because he was a member of the A.A. and was in honour bound to reimburse the A.A. so far as he recovered the costs against the other side.

Lewis v. Averay (No. 2),
[1973] 2 All E.R. 229; [1973] 1 W.L.R. 510; 117 S.J. 188 (C.A.)

The respondent, successful both in the Court of Appeal and the House of Lords (in both of which the appellant was legally aided) applied for an order under s. 1 (1) of the 1964 Act that his costs on the appeal should be paid out of the legal aid fund (see DAVIES V. TAYLOR, above, p. A37). He was insured under a motor policy and his insurers would pay his costs.

HELD: an order should be made. The costs were "incurred by him in the proceedings" within s. 1 (1) even though the insurers agreed to pay them, unless there was an agreement between him and his solicitors that he would not pay their costs; it had not been proved there was. The fact that the order would benefit the insurers did not prevent it from being "just and equitable". The court had a very wide discretion under the Act; success in the appeal alone (contrary to the view expressed by the Court of Appeal in CLIFFORD V. WALKER, [1972] 2 All E.R. 806 (above,

PAGE

661 p. A54) could be a sufficient justification for an order. But the court
cont. should not usually give its reasons.

Davies v. Taylor (No. 2),
[1973] 1 All E.R. 959; [1973] 2 W.L.R. 610; 117 S.J. 246 (H.L.)

See also two applications similarly dealt with on the same occasion: SHILOH SPINNERS, LTD. V. HARDING (NO. 2) and O'BRIEN V. ROBINSON (NO. 2), [1973] 1 All E.R. 966 and 969. For s. 1(1) of the 1964 Act see now s. 13 (1) of the 1974 Act.

661 **After Edwards v. Edwards add.—**

Section 1(7)(b) of the 1949 Act is re-enacted as s. 2(5)(b) of the 1974 Act.

663 **After Daley v. Diggers, Ltd. add.—**

The section of the 1974 Act are as follows:—

1949 Act	*1974 Act*
1(7)(b)	2(5)(b)
2(2)	8(1)
3(7)	9(9)

663 **After Gibbs v. Gibbs add.—**

Paragraph 4(1) of the Third Schedule to the 1949 Act is now replaced by paragraph 4(1) of the Second Schedule to the 1974 Act.

668 **Road Traffic Act 1972, s. 144**

In sub-s. (2) after para. (e) insert the following paragraph: "(f) to a vehicle which is made available by the Secretary of State to any person, body or local authority in pursuance of s. 11 or s. 13 of the National Health Service Reorganisation Act 1973 at a time when it is being used in accordance with the terms on which it is so made available". (National Health Service (Vehicles) Order 1974, S.I. 1974 No. 168, art. 4).

668 **After heading "'Using' a motor vehicle" add.—**

The defendant was being brought home from work in his own car driven by a woman who was not his servant when an accident occurred. Neither of them was insured. The defendant was charged with "using" his car when not insured, contrary to s. 201 of the Road Traffic Act 1960 (now s. 143 of the 1972 Act). The magistrates dismissed the charge on the ground that the meaning of "use" should not be extended beyond driving and that the charge should have been one of "permitting".

HELD: this was not right. The word "use" is wider than "drive". The defendant was using his own car for his own purposes and in person in being driven home, though the driver was somebody else.

Cobb v. Williams,
[1973] R.T.R. 113 (Div. Ct.)

A co-partner does not "use" a vehicle merely because it is driven by his partner on partnership business.

Garrett v. Hooper,
[1973] R.T.R. 1 (Div. Ct.)

672 **After Law v. Thomas add.—**

Followed and applied in BINKS V. DEPARTMENT OF ENVIRONMENT, [1975] R.T.R. 318 (an excise case).

PAGE

673 **After Brown v. Abbott add.—**

The defendants were prosecuted for using a motor vehicle on a road without insurance. The vehicle was a mini which the defendants had bought as scrap and had rebuilt for autocross racing, removing the windows, passenger seat and number plates and substituting a rev. counter for the speedometer. They towed it on public roads to a meeting, one defendant driving the towing vehicle and the other steering the mini. They contested the charge on the ground that the mini was not "intended or adapted for use on roads" within s. 253(1) of the 1960 Act (now s. 190 (1) of the Road Traffic Act 1972), since they had no intention of using it on roads nor had they adapted it for that purpose.

HELD: a car does not cease to be a vehicle intended for use on roads merely because its present owner sees no prospect of driving it on a road under its own power. The mini had retained its character as a motor car intended to run on roads and was within s. 253(1).

Nichol v. Leach,
[1972] R.T.R. 476 (Div. Ct.)

BURNS V. CURRELL (p. 672) and BROWN V. ABBOTT (p. 673) were not cited.

687 **After note following Morris v. Williams add.—**

The defendant gave permission to Jarvis to borrow his car and use it provided he insured it. Jarvis failed to insure it and was convicted of using the car without insurance. The defendant was charged with "permitting" Jarvis to use the car uninsured.

HELD: he was not guilty. Permission given subject to a condition which is unfulfilled is no permission at all.

Newbury v. Davis,
[1974] R.T.R. 367 (Div. Ct.)

690 **Add to note following Windle v. Dunning.—**

Also BALFOUR BEATTY V. GRINDLEY, [1975] R.T.R. 156 and HOWARD V. G. T. JONES & CO., LTD., [1975] R.T.R. 150.

692 **After Bugge v. Taylor add.—**

An alley 8′ 6″ wide led to a path 10′ wide. Together they joined two public roads, and though contained within council property, were used by pedestrians as a short cut between the two roads. The Council did not object to people using it in this way.

HELD: the evidence was quite sufficient to entitle the jury to make the finding that the public had access and that the alley and path were a "road".

R. v. Shaw,
[1974] R.T.R. 225 (C.A.)

695 **After Chapman v. Parlby add.—**

A local authority made a traffic control order prohibiting waiting in a road giving access to a car park. There was an adjoining loading area and a cul-de-sac, not separated from the road by any physical barrier: the double yellow lines on the road included the area and cul-de-sac. The defendants were lessees of a shop from the authority on terms which gave them some right over the cul-de-sac but not a right to exclude the

PAGE

695 *cont.* public. The defendants parked a vehicle in the cul-de-sac and were prosecuted for contravening the traffic order. They contended that the cul-de-sac was not a "road".

HELD: following BUCHANAN V. M.I.B. (above) the test was whether there was any physical obstruction for the public to overcome or any prohibition express or implied to public access. The magistrates were justified in holding on the evidence that the cul-de-sac was a road.

Houghton v. Schofield,
[1973] Crim L.R. 126 (Div. Ct.)

698 **Road Traffic Act 1972, s. 145**

At the end of sub-s. (2) the following words are added by s. 20(1) of the Road Traffic Act 1974: "and being a member of the Motor Insurers Bureau, a company limited by guarantee and incorporated under the Companies Act 1929 on the 14th June 1946".

In sub-s. (3)(a) insert the words "in Great Britain" after the words "on a road". Add after paragraph (a) the following paragraph:

"(aa) must insure him or them in respect of any liability which may be incurred by him or them in respect of the use of the vehicle and of any trailer, whether or not coupled, in the territory other than Great Britain and Gibraltar of each of the member states of the communities according to the law on compulsory insurance against civil liability in respect of the use of vehicles of the State where the liability may be incurred; and". (Both amendments made by the Motor Vehicles (Compulsory Insurance) (No. 2) Regulations 1973, S.I. 1973 No. 2143).

698 **After note following s. 145 add.—**

SUBSECTION (3)(a): CONSORTIUM

The husband's right to sue for damages for loss of consortium, loss of his wife's society and services is a "liability" which is required by law to be covered by insurance, being a liability "in respect of . . . bodily injury to any person caused by, or arising out of, the use of the vehicle on a road" within s. 145(3)(a) of the Road Traffic Act 1972.

Ladd v. Jones,
[1975] R.T.R. 67 (Lawson, J.)

709 **After note following Albert v. M.I.B. add.—**

The plaintiff, a fellow employee of the defendant's, travelled to and from work in the defendant's car under an arrangement whereby passengers travelled at their own risk. He was injured in an accident in 1970 caused by the defendant's negligent driving. The judge held, following ALBERT V. M.I.B. (main volume, p. 709) that the plaintiff was being carried for hire or reward. It was argued for the plaintiff that as the effect of ss. 201 and 203 of the Road Traffic Act 1960 was that the defendant must be insured against injury to passengers the arrangement that the plaintiff travelled at his own risk was void either for illegality or as being contrary to public policy.

HELD: it was not illegal because the car was not a public service vehicle and s. 151 of the 1960 Act (main volume, p. 185) did not apply; (2) it was not contrary to public policy. There may be very good reasons for allowing this sort of arrangement when the vehicle is not a public service vehicle. Judgment for the defendant.

Bridgeford v. Weston,
[1975] R.T.R. 189 (Waller, J.)

PAGE

716 **After heading "Temporary cover note" add.—**

Roberts, a hire-car driver, made an agreement with Davies, who ran a hire-car booking office, that he would drive Davies's car when required on bookings provided by Davies, who would ensure that Roberts was covered by Davies's insurance. As the car, when the agreement was made, was insured only for named drivers of whom Roberts was not one, they went to the insurance brokers through whom Davies's insurance was placed, where Davies in Roberts's presence asked the brokers that the policy should be varied to cover any driver. The brokers telephoned the insurers who specifically authorised them to give insurance cover for any driver of the car. The brokers thereupon issued a 60-day cover note to Davies providing for such cover. The insurers later decided not to provide "any driver" cover but their letters to the brokers on the subject were delayed by a postal strike and did not reach them. More than 60 days after the issue of the cover-note Roberts was stopped and charged with driving when uninsured.

HELD, ON APPEAL BY CASE STATED: Roberts was rightly convicted. The Road Traffic Act 1960, s. 201, requires that there shall be a policy of insurance in force in relation to the persons using the vehicle. The cover note was in itself a policy of insurance (though an insurance certificate is not) albeit a temporary one and there was a certificate printed on it; but the policy had not been amended when the cover note expired and did not cover Roberts. The telephone conversation between brokers and insurers did not amount to an oral variation of the existing written policy. The fact that the insurers might in the circumstances have been estopped as against Roberts from denying that he was entitled to be indemnified did not make up for the lack of a policy on the relevant date so far as s. 201 was concerned, since a policy is something which has to be in writing and requires stamping, and no amendment to include Roberts expressly had been done when the cover-note expired.

Roberts v. Warne,
[1973] R.T.R. 217 (Div. Ct.)

724 **After heading "Cancellation" add.—**

The plaintiffs' fleet of 82 vehicles was insured under a policy issued by the defendant underwriters containing a provision that they were entitled to cancel the policy on seven days' notice and in such event they would refund a proportion of the premium on surrender of the insurance certificate. The defendants supplied the plaintiffs with six copies of the certificate all identical except for the numbers. After receiving notice of cancellation the plaintiffs returned three of the copies but could not find the others. The defendants refused to make a refund of premium until all should be returned.

HELD: the plaintiffs were entitled to a refund. The defendants had not issued six certificates but one only with five additional copies. By returning the certificate numbered 1 the plaintiff had complied with the terms of the policy. The provisions of the Road Traffic Act (i.e. ss. 147 and 149 of the 1972 Act) were irrelevant.

J. H. Moore & Co. v. Crowe,
[1972] 2 Lloyd's Rep. 563 (Mayor's and City of London Court)

PAGE

729 Road Traffic Act 1972, s. 151

In sub-s. (1)(b) delete from the words "the certificate" to the end and substitute the words "any certificate of insurance or security delivered in respect of that policy or security, as the case may be, under s. 147 of this Act, or where no such certificate was delivered under the said section the following particulars, that is to say, the registration mark or other identifying particulars of the vehicle concerned, the number or other identifying particulars of the insurance policy issued in respect of the vehicle, the name of the insurer and the period of the insurance cover" (Motor Vehicles (Compulsory Insurance) (No. 2) Regulations 1973, S.I. 1973 No. 2143).

730 Motor Insurers Bureau Agreement

In respect of accidents occurring on or after December 1, 1972, the 1972 agreement is replaced by a new agreement of November 22, 1972, to deal with the extension of compulsory third party insurance to passenger risks. The only material difference between the two agreements is in clause 6 which in the 1972 agreement is as follows:—

EXEMPTIONS

6.(1) M.I.B. shall not incur any liability under Clause 2 of this Agreement in a case where—

(*a*) the claim arises out of the use of a vehicle owned by or in the possession of the Crown, except where any other person has undertaken responsibility for the existence of a contract of insurance under Part VI of the Road Traffic Act 1972 (whether or not the person or persons liable be in fact covered by a contract of insurance) or where the liability is in fact covered by a contract of insurance;

(*b*) the claim arises out of the use of a vehicle the use of which is not required to be covered by a contract of insurance by virtue of section 144 of the Road Traffic Act 1972, unless the use is in fact covered by such a contract;

(*c*) at the time of the accident the person suffering death or bodily injury in respect of which the claim is made was allowing himself to be carried in a vehicle and—

(i) knew or had reason to believe that the vehicle had been taken without the consent of the owner or other lawful authority except in a case where—

(A) he believed or had reason to believe that he had lawful authority to be carried or that he would have had the owner's consent if the owner had known of his being carried and the circumstances of his carriage; or

(B) he had learned of the circumstances of the taking of the vehicle since the commencement of the journey and it would be unreasonable to expect him to have alighted from the vehicle; or

(ii) being the owner of or being a person using the vehicle, he was using or causing or permitting the vehicle to be used without there being in force in relation to such use a contract of insurance as would comply with Part VI of the Road Traffic Act 1972, knowing or having reason to believe that no such contract was in force.

(2) The exemption specified in sub-paragraph (1)(*c*) of this Clause shall apply only in a case where the judgment in respect of which the claim against M.I.B. is made was obtained in respect of a relevant liability incurred by the owner or a person using the vehicle in which the person who suffered death or bodily injury was being carried.

PAGE

730 (3) For the purposes of these exemptions—
cont.
(*a*) a vehicle which has been unlawfully removed from the possession of the Crown shall be taken to continue in that possession whilst it is kept so removed;
(*b*) references to a person being carried in a vehicle include references to his being carried in or upon or entering or getting on to or alighting from the vehicle;
(*c*) "owner" in relation to a vehicle which is the subject of a hiring agreement or a hire-purchase agreement, means the person in possession of the vehicle under that agreement.

References in the 1971 Agreement to the Road Traffic Act 1960 have been amended in the 1972 Agreement to the appropriate provisions of the Road Traffic Act 1972.

739 **Add to the note "The Domestic Agreement".—**

The Road Traffic Act 1974 by s. 20 now requires all authorised insurers as defined in s. 145(2) of the 1972 Act to be members of Motor Insurers Bureau.

740 **Untraced Motorists Agreement 1969**

In respect of accidents occurring on or after December 1, 1972, the 1969 Agreement has been replaced by a new agreement dated November 22, 1972. No material alterations have been made to the Notes of the 1969 Agreement on pp. 740–741 of the main volume. The principal alteration in the agreement is an addition to cl. 1 so as to exclude passenger claims where the passenger knew that the vehicle had been taken without the owner's consent or being the owner or user of the vehicle was using it or causing or permitting it to be used uninsured.

741 **After Untraced Motorists agreement add.—**

The plaintiff, a bus conductor, was injured when the bus pulled up sharply. He claimed damages from his employers on the ground that the driver was negligent, but they denied liability; they said the accident was caused by the negligence of a motorist who could not be identified or traced. The plaintiff applied to M.I.B. for an award under the 1969 (untraced drivers) agreement. After investigation M.I.B. decided that no award should be made because the plaintiff had not satisfied cl. 1(1)(c). He then began proceedings in the County Court against his employers and M.I.B., alleging a failure by M.I.B. to compensate him in accordance with the 1969 agreement. The County Court judge ordered the claim against M.I.B. to be struck out on the ground that it disclosed no cause of action.

HELD, ON APPEAL: the judge was right. The agreement is enforceable by the Minister and (by consent of M.I.B.) by an applicant, but only in accordance with the terms of the agreement. An award under cl. 3 in favour of an applicant is expressly made subject to the provisions of the following clauses, including cl. 7, which prescribes what M.I.B. has to do and, when done, requiring M.I.B. to decide whether to make an award. The process under cl. 7 is subject to a right of appeal under cl. 11, but if there is no award there is no right to payment. M.I.B.'s decision to reject the application was in fulfilment of the terms of the agreement and not a repudiation of it. An applicant cannot bring an action against

PAGE

741 M.I.B. alleging breach of the agreement upon a basis of fact which is
cont. reserved by the agreement for M.I.B.'s decision.

Persson v. London Country Buses,
[1974] 1 All E.R. 1251; [1974] 1 W.L.R. 569; [1974] 1 Lloyd's Rep. 415 (C.A.)

745 **After Locker & Woolf, Ltd. v. Western Australian Ins. Co. add.—**

The plaintiff company owned and ran a club and casino and was itself controlled and directed by S. and his wife. In 1967 the defendant insurers issued a policy covering the contents against fire risks, extended on renewal to cover the company's buildings. On June 14, 1969 S. was arrested on a charge of handling stolen goods and on November 28, 1969 was committed for trial. The policy fell due for renewal on April 20, 1970; when renewing S. did not disclose his arrest and committal to the insurers. On June 22, 1970, he was convicted and fined £2000. On September 14, 1970, there was a fire at the club premises causing £27,024 damage. The insurers, after investigation in which they learned of S.'s prosecution and conviction declared the policy void on the ground of material non-disclosure when the policy was renewed in April 1970.

HELD: there had been a material non-disclosure entitling the insurers to avoid the policy. The duty to disclose material facts arises outside the contract of insurance and not by way of implied term. The test of materiality was whether the facts would, on a fair consideration of the evidence, influence a reasonable insurer to decline the risk. Whether a particular circumstance is material or not is a question of fact in which the moral integrity of the proposer is important. S. should, before renewal in April 1970, have disclosed that he had committed the crime referred to; even if he had subsequently been acquitted he ought to have disclosed the fact of his arrest, charge and committal, but not if he had been acquitted before the renewal.

March Cabaret Club and Casino, Ltd. v. London Assurance,
[1975] 1 Lloyd's Rep. 169 (May, J.)

747 **After Glickman v. Lancs. & General Assurance Co. add.—**

The duty is on the assured to disclose any material information which he has, and it is only if, as the cases indicate, the insurers are put on enquiry about some particular matter that it can be said that they have waived the obligation, the requirement, as to disclosure. As Banks, L.J. put it in the case of MANN MACNEAL V. CAPITAL AND COUNTIES INS. CO., [1912] K.B. 300, quoting Lord Esher: ". . . it is not necessary to disclose minutely every material fact; assuming that there is a material fact which [the assured] is bound to disclose, the rule is satisfied if he discloses sufficient to call the attention of the underwriters in such a manner they can see that if they require further information they ought to ask for it."

Arterial Caravans, Ltd. v. Yorkshire Insurance Co.,
[1973] 1 Lloyd's Rep. 169 (Chapman, J.)

760 **After Farra v. Hetherington add.—**

Promissory Declaration

Miss Kirkbride filled in a proposal form for insurance of her car. In answer to the question "Will the car to your knowledge be driven by any

PAGE

760 *cont.* person under 25 years of age?" she put merely "Yes, self". She signed the usual declaration at the end of the form containing the words "this declaration signed by me is promissory". The policy when issued provided that the underwriters would not be liable in respect of loss whilst the car was "being driven by or in charge for that purpose of any person in whose record there is to the knowledge of the policy holder a prejudice existing such as would amount to material information to be known to the underwriters". On an occasion when she intended to visit a theatre club she allowed her younger brother to drive there in her car on an arrangement that she would use it to drive him back at the end of the visit. Her brother drove the car there, parked it and handed her the keys. During the evening the car was stolen and not recovered. The underwriters refused to meet the loss.

HELD: they were not entitled to decline liability under the policy, because (1) on the facts Miss Kirkbride's brother was not in charge of the car when it was stolen, since the purpose for which he had driven the car had come to an end and Miss Kirkbride was herself at the club; (2) the use of the word "promissory" in the declaration did not mean that she was warranting that the situation implied or expressed in the proposal form would continue into the future: all it meant was, "At the time of signing the form those are my intentions". When she signed the proposal form Miss Kirkbride did not intend that the car would be driven by anyone under the age of 25 other than herself.

Kirkbride v. Donner,
[1974] 1 Lloyd's Rep. 549 (Mayor's and City of London Court)

774 After note following R. v. Wilkins add.—

A motorist pushing his car with his shoulder against the door pillar and both feet on the road, controlling movement by his hand on the steering wheel, is not "driving" within the meaning of the Road Traffic Act 1972.

R. v. MacDonagh,
[1974] Q.B. 448; [1974] 2 All E.R. 257; [1974] 2 W.L.R. 529; 118 S.J. 529 (C.A.)

807 After Louden v. British Merchants Ins. Co. add.—

After drinking a pint and a half of lager with friends the defender gave them a lift in his car. On a straight section of a dual carriageway road the car crossed the central intersection and collided with a sign. The two passengers were killed. The defender's motor policy contained a condition exempting the insurers from liability for any claim arising when the insured was driving and was under the influence of intoxicating liquor. The defender had signed a declaration when proposing for insurance that he was a total abstainer from birth and would notify the insurers if this ceased to apply.

HELD: (1) the admitted consumption of lager and the erratic and unexplained behaviour of the car justified a conclusion that at the moment of the accident the defender was under the influence of intoxicating liquor, applying the test in MAIR's and LOUDEN's cases (main volume, p. 807). The condition exempted the insurers from liability; (2) the declaration did not merely create an obligation to notify the insurer if the defender ceased to be a total abstainer. To get cover he had declared he was a

PAGE

807 *cont.* total abstainer from birth and when the accident happened he was in breach of that declaration. The insurers were not liable under the policy.

Kennedy v. Smith
1974 S.L.T. (Notes) 18.

807 **Greenleaf Associated, Ltd. v. Monksfield**

Reported at [1972] R.T.R. 451 and [1972] 2 Lloyd's Rep. 79.

807 **After Greenleaf Associated, Ltd. v. Monksfield add.—**

Motor car

The defendant was insured for use of his motor car by a policy which extended cover to him additionally against third party claims arising from accidents caused by or in connection with "the driving by the insured of any motor car . . . not belonging to him . . .". He was driving a Ford Transit van not belonging to him when there was an accident in which the plaintiff was injured. The defendant's insurers refused to indemnify him on the ground that the van was not a "motor car". The defendant relied on the definition in s. 253(2) of the Road Traffic Act 1960 (now s. 190(2) of the 1972 Act) "'motor car' means a mechanically propelled vehicle, not being a motor cycle or invalid carriage, which is constructed itself to carry a load or passengers and the weight of which unladen . . . does not exceed three tons".

HELD: the van was a motor car. The words had to be considered in the context of motor insurance. If motor insurers wished to put some meaning on words like "motor car" other than those contained in the Road Traffic Act they should make it abundantly clear in the policy; if they failed to do so the words would be deemed to have the statutory meanings.

Laurence v. Davies,
[1972] 2 Lloyd's Rep. 231 (Dunn, J.)

815 **After John Edwards & Co. v. Motor Union add.—**

As a term of a contract to perform cleaning services for the Ford Motor Company, Cameron Industrial Services agreed to indemnify Fords against all claims made by (*inter alios*) their own employees arising from negligence on the part of Ford's employees. Morris, an employee of Cameron was injured by the negligence of Roberts, an employee of Fords. His claim was met by Fords, who claimed indemnity from Cameron. Admitting their liability to indemnify Fords, Cameron sued Roberts, claiming to do so in right of subrogation to the rights of Fords to claim against their employee as in LISTER's case. Evidence was given that Fords never sued their servants because to do so would be to court industrial action in the form of strikes: serious industrial repercussions would follow if they entered into contracts under the terms of which their servants might be sued by others in their name.

HELD: a right of subrogation arises from the very nature of the contract of indemnity itself and not from any implied term in the contract, but it can be excluded expressly or by implication. In the present case of an agreement operative in an industrial setting in which employers never

PAGE

815 sue their servants because of likely industrial repercussions a term of the
cont. contract was to be implied that the right of subrogation was excluded.

Morris v. Ford Motor Co.,
[1973] Q.B. 792; [1973] 2 All E.R. 1084; [1973] 2 W.L.R. 843; 117 S.J. 393 (C.A.)

818 **After Coote and Green, Ltd. v. Tyrrell add.—**

The owner of a car damaged in an accident took it to repairers telling them it was comprehensively insured and asking for an estimate of the cost of repair. The estimate was sent to him a few days later. He also notified his insurers who sent their assessor to see the repairers. Agreement was reached between assessor and insurer on the cost of repairs and a printed form was filled in by the assessor which *inter alia* notified the repairers of the need for them to collect the £25 excess from the owner. The repairs were then carried out and an invoice sent by the repairers to the insurers, though without a signed satisfaction note from the owner, as he was not satisfied with the work done. He had some work done to the car elsewhere (the cost of which he deducted from the excess) and then took the signed satisfaction note to the repairers. By that time the insurers had gone into liquidation and the repairers were not paid. They sued the owner for the whole cost of the repairs.

HELD: there were two contracts involved, one between the repairers and the insurers whereby the insurers undertook to pay for the repairs and one between the owner and repairers (to be implied from his having taken the vehicle to them for repair) by which the repairers undertook to carry out the work expeditiously (as in CHARNOCK V. LIVERPOOL CORPORATION, main volume, p. 819). But there was nothing from which in the contract between the owner and repairers a term could be implied that the owner had a liability to pay for the repairs beyond the amount of the excess. The facts of the case were clearly parallel with those in GODFREY DAVIS V. CULLING (main volume, p. 817) and, COOTE AND GREEN V. TYRRELL (main volume, p. 818) and there was nothing in the judgments in CHARNOCK's case to controvert the principles applied in either of those cases.

Brown and Davies, Ltd. v. Galbraith,
[1972] 3 All E.R. 31; [1972] 1 W.L.R. 997; [1972] R.T.R. 523 (C.A.)

825 **After Greenwood v. Martin's Bank add.—**

Insurance Companies Act 1958

The defendant company ran an association to protect the interests of motorists. Members could pay an annual sum and, subject to the decision of a committee could be provided with a chauffeur if they became legally unable to drive because of, e.g., becoming disqualified on conviction of a road traffic offence. The decision of the committee was final and an applicant had to satisfy certain requirements but the committee's discretion was not absolute: if the member fulfilled the requirements he was entitled to the services offered by the association.

HELD: the defendants were an insurance company to which the Insurance Companies Act 1958 applied.

PAGE

825 **Department of Trade and Industry v. St. Christopher Motorist**
cont. **Association, Ltd.,**

[1974] 1 All E.R. 395; [1974] 1 W.L.R. 99; [1974] 1 Lloyd's Rep. 17 (Ch.D.)

825 **After note following Beresford v. Royal Ins. Co. add.—**

The plaintiffs arranged with the defendants, who were hauliers, to carry two pieces of machinery each weighing 25 tons from Stockton to Hull. The defendants sent two articulated lorries each of 10 tons unladen weight to collect the machinery which was loaded on the lorries in the presence of the plaintiffs' transport manager, who knew that when loaded each vehicle would weigh 35 tons. He was aware of the regulation in the Motor Vehicles (Construction and Use) Regulations 1966 limiting the permissible loaded weight of an articulated lorry to 30 tons. On the journey one of the lorries overturned damaging the machinery.

HELD: the plaintiffs were barred from suing the defendants for the damage. Even if the contract was lawful when made (in that it could have been performed by using the right kind of vehicle) the performance of it was illegal. The plaintiffs' transport manager who knew the weight of the two loads and the regulations failed to stop the loading when he went to watch it being done: he was a participator in the illegality.

Ashmore, Benson, Pease & Co., Ltd. v. A. V. Dawson, Ltd.,

[1973] 2 All E.R. 856; [1973] 1 W.L.R. 828; [1973] R.T.R. 473 (C.A.)

842 **After Mason v. Burningham add.—**

Bennett wishing to have some work done to a car to prepare it for sale entrusted it to Searle to do the work. Searle used the car for his own purposes and in doing so damaged it. He wrongfully "sold" it in its damaged state to Harper who in good faith paid him £75 for it. Harper spent £226 on it to put it in good order and then sold it for £450 to a finance company. When Searle's misdealing with the car was discovered the police seized the car and brought interpleader proceedings to determine the ownership. The judge ordered the car to be delivered up to Bennett and held that Harper was not entitled to be paid by Bennett for the £226 worth of work done to the car.

HELD: the judge should have required Bennett to pay Harper the £226 as a condition of being given delivery of the car. The principle that lay to hand to meet the case was derived from the law of restitution—that the owners should not be allowed to enrich themselves at the expense of a person who has done work to a property of which he honestly believes himself to be the owner.

Greenwood v. Bennett,

[1973] Q.B. 195; [1972] 3 All E.R. 586; [1972] 3 W.L.R. 691; [1972] R.T.R. 535 (C.A.)

851 **After Bishopsgate Motor Finance v. Transport Brakes add.—**

At 7 in the morning of February 13 Cocks bought a silver candelabra from a stall-holder who was just erecting his stall in the New Caledonian Market, Bermondsey. The candelabra had been stolen from the plaintiff by a person unknown.

HELD: Cocks did not obtain a good title. Though the market overt

PAGE

851 rule extended to statutory markets such as the New Caledonian a sale
cont. which would give a good title against the true owner must be made "between the rising of the sun and the going down of the same" (Coke, 2 Inst. 713). Sunrise being at 8.19 a.m. on February 13, the sale was not one made in market overt.

Reid v. Metropolitan Police Commissioner,
[1973] Q.B. 551; [1973] 2 All E.R. 97; [1973] 2 W.L.R. 576; [1973] Lloyd's Rep. 518 (C.A.)

Printed in Great Britain by William Clowes & Sons, Limited, London, Beccles and Colchester